Raku Pottery

Robert Piepenburg

Raku Pottery

Collier Books
A Division of Macmillan Publishing Co., Inc.
New York

Collier Macmillan Publishers
London

To Wendy and Matthew

The translation of the Rikyu poem is from *Cha-No-Yu The Japanese Tea Ceremony* by A. L. Sadler. Used by permission of Charles E. Tuttle Co., Inc., Tokyo.

Macmillan Publishing Co., Inc.
866 Third Avenue, New York, N.Y. 10022
Collier Macmillan Canada, Ltd.
Library of Congress Catalog Card Number: 75-188768

Raku Pottery is also published in a hardcover edition
by Macmillan Publishing Co., Inc.

First Collier Books Edition 1976

10 9 8 7 6 5 4 3 2

Printed in the United States of America

Contents

Foreword

AS A POTTER...

Many potters, and I include myself among them, find it easy to function in the world of mute arts; but in the scholar's or poet's world of verbal arts, we become ill at ease. In teaching pottery I am aware of speech as a vehicle for communication, and the fact that it is difficult to find the right words to express those usually unspoken feelings of relatedness that working with clay can produce and extend.

If I am to be a good midwife, as teacher and author, I must enter into a dialogue with meanings felt and meaning expression. As a teacher it is easy to explain and demonstrate ceramic techniques. But when it comes to the more subtle areas of personal development and individual involvement, I must hope propinquity will awaken student perceptions. Because the reader cannot be with me in the classroom or studio, and we cannot work together and exchange rhythms, ideas, and a "sense of life," I will have to try to verbally clarify the dualism between the nonverbal and the verbal.

Spoken words are sounds; written words are pictures or symbols that name, describe, or explain concepts and objects. Ultimately, words separate; they are objects describing still more objects. Nonverbal communication is a direct experience, an experience where subject and object are united, without mediator, on the bridge of the senses. Words are experienced in a linear fashion, but pottery is total and simultaneous in its impact.

Potting is more than technique; it is more than the forming of clay and the making of objects. It is, in many ways, the forming of the self. I do not know to what extent we become aware of our selves through daily activities. I have never before labored to define, examine, or bring this awareness from a preconscious to a conscious level. I have only felt it— sometimes fleetingly, sometimes passionately. I have tried to define and develop my own thinking—to enunciate how potting is into my life. Just as you might unroll a scroll to see its entire surface, writing *Raku Pottery* has helped me to unroll my thoughts and lay them out where I can disclose myself to myself. Hopefully it will be of some help to you also.

An inquiry into the essence of life is part of Zen Buddhist philosophy. It is no accident that raku developed with the growth of the Japanese tea ceremony, an aspect of Zen. Zen has never made a distinction in the arts; a poem, a drawing, a pot, or a musical arrangement are equally beautiful. And a good pot is no more accidental than a good poem.

Raku comes from a background of universal human experience and offers the potter spiritual insight into himself as well as his craft. As potters, we can only hope to widen our consciousness so that our work can have a deeper meaning. Working with clay can often satisfy an inner need. I know a woman who was a professional painter until she had a child; afterward, she could no longer work on a two-dimensional canvas and turned to pottery where she felt in touch with a life-giving substance.

I have noticed very sincere and sensitive potters examining my work. They quietly look inside the piece, turn it over, inspect the foot, follow the glaze, and then carefully return the pot to rest. I often sense that they are looking for some insights into the maker. With their minds attuned to their senses they scrutinize the exposed and the hidden identity of the maker and try to touch his feelings and personality. When they succeed nothing is concealed—least of all my pleasure at the moment. Others will examine a pot not for any insight into its maker, but in terms of its form, size, texture, and, most of all, color. They do not understand that it reflects human experience, they are looking for something to fill an aesthetic or functional need. Raku is a poor choice for casseroles and makes leaky flower vases; it is pottery that is apart from a utilitarian function. Raku must be approached with a different criterion in mind.

Robert Piepenburg, hand built raku plate 18" wide. To allow for wall mounting, holes were made on the underside of the piece with a bent section of brazing rod.

If someone were to ask me why I, as a potter, like a particular piece of pottery, I might reply that when I look at the pot, I see an aspect of myself shared and reflected by the potter. As I become more involved in pottery, I experience myself more fully, and I am better able to understand and appreciate the experiences of others. Usually, I do not like a pot because of some lack of rapport. My approval of a pot is partially dependent on my understanding of its artist, but more so to the extent that I have experienced the same intuitions the artist is trying to express. There is, however, no absolute scale.

Our work represents us. It reflects our vision and spirit. It echoes our moods and experiences. Pottery is not created by the hands alone but by the entire body and being. It is not unusual to describe pottery in human terms, to speak of a thin lip, a narrow neck, a rounded shoulder, a tumescent belly, a masculine form, a feminine form, or even a tear of glaze—to use terms such as whimpering, timid, sensual, pretentious, or sophisticated. In China the T'ang potters regarded the unglazed foot of a pot as being naked, and thereby without concealment of its maker. I think an intuitive approach to reviewing and evaluating pottery is far more honest than a dealer's cold-blooded pricing or a collector's acquisitory analysis. Pots express an intimacy and can impart the qualities we value in people.

Our pottery gives testimony to ourselves. To a potter, education is really self-education; it is the continual revelation of oneself by oneself. Each time the potter transforms a mass of clay the clay is transforming the potter; his creating is the searching and finding of meaning; an attempt to unite man and his being. I often believe that a beautiful pot achieves that goal.

It is very difficult to sell or give away a beautiful pot. They should be kept around, if not as reminders of the enlightenment they provide, then for their expression of a moment. But, if they are to break or be given away, we must remember that they are really impermanent objects and have their immortality in their creator and the visions that evolved in him during the fever of their birth.

A potter must continue to search for his own meaning. The act of preparing the clay by mixing and wedging is not as important as the act of preparing ourselves. We want to know what we are going to produce with the clay and with ourselves. Like a bud growing from a stem and reaching for the eternal light of the sun, the potter sits at his wheel with both clay and being "on center," knowing that, as he opens and pulls up the spinning clay, growth will take place for the clay and for himself. If the clay form were to mature only to wobble and collapse, a change would still have occurred within the potter.

A question often asked is, What is the distinction that separates pottery from ceramic sculpture? Ceramic sculpture has an integral life of its own. It is concerned with exploring and creating new or different areas of artistic communication and expression. Often it is created by either a subtractive or additive process (the subtraction or addition of material such as clay, metal, or plastic). Pottery is growth by evolution—the potter generally creates by molding his clay from one shape to another. Whether or not this is a valid distinction is really unimportant to the potter or the sculptor. What is of relevance is the transformation of *self* that takes place during the engagement with the clay. The potter is like the clay, he is formed by development and evolution.

The Zen precept of growth is that yielding contributes to strength, and resistance contributes to weakness. If this philosophy is applied in the studio to the clay and the potter, the strength of both will remain in the pot. The potter and the pot are like many living things in nature. The process of inner growth is the process of life. The concatenation of the seed, the tree, and the fruit are like the pot and the potter—they grow from the center. The concrescence that takes place between pot and potter defies analysis; the spirit flows between the form and its maker.

The skills and techniques of the potter are decisive only in that they must be mastered until they are intuitive; they must be assimilated, be part of the center, to be effective. They serve as vehicles for feelings and creation. The potter, like the dancer, cannot be freely responsive to the moment until he has mastered and subordinated the techniques of his discipline. Students often become overly enthusiastic about the process of throwing and make a whole raft of dull, lifeless pots. Technique alone does not provide the substance and the vitality of life. There are times when I feel complete but leave the potter's wheel tired and unhappy. At other times I approach the wheel sensing frustration and find the clay pulling me together. There are times when the clay and potter are at odds, when the potter struggles with his own identity through the clay, but these unproductive sessions are more than compensated for by those precious moments when the potter and clay are in harmony.

The harmonious dialogue between pot and potter during the stages of conception is what gives pottery life and spirit. For this life-spirit to exist the potter must give all of himself; and it is in the act of giving that love resides.

R.P.

Royal Oak, Michigan
1972

Raku
Pottery

Charles Sharbaugh (student), wheel form with slab collar, 19" high.

1

Raku
In Japan

A DESCRIPTION AND HISTORY

To fully understand raku, we cannot embrace one phase but must look for a kinship with all its phases. One way of defining raku, other than as a type of pottery preferred by Japanese tea masters, is to say that it is a low-temperature technique of firing porous, low bisque fired pottery, usually bearing a lead glaze. The technique generally involves a placement of pottery in a pre-heated kiln with tongs and removal from the kiln, again with tongs, while the pot is still glowing hot.

One story explaining the introduction of tongs into the raku firing process centers around one of Japan's many natural disasters. During the frenzied rebuilding, Korean potters in Japan were called on to produce enormous quantities of roof tile. In their haste, they began to use tongs to remove the still-hot tiles from the kiln, and discovered that the tiles did not crack or break. The clay's ability to withstand this shocking move from the hot kiln to the cool air was attributed to the high sand content in the clay. Japanese potters had long since claimed most of the good clay deposits, forcing the Koreans to work sub-standard clay containing large proportions of sand. It is known that earthenware clay bodies were used exactly as they came from the natural clay deposits and it is very possible that a raku clay body may have been discovered in this way.

Tea Bowls

With the exception of a few contemporary potters, the raku clay pottery of Japan, particularly the tea bowls, are usually hand-built pieces. The hand building of raku is traditional; raku was valued and favored for its tasteful unpretentiousness which is associated with and achieved by hand building. The history of raku goes back almost four hundred years, but even today there are Japanese potters who wheel form tea bowls and then hand form the same bowl when the clay is leather hard. This hand forming encouraged the valued irregularity of shape.

Tea bowls are seldom made perfectly round. They are usually designed to conform to being held in both hands, since that is the way they are normally held when they are used for drinking tea. To achieve this some potters take the not quite dry, leather-hard bowls and gently toss them into the air catching them in both hands. The top edges of the

Ray Kahmeyer, paddled wheel-thrown raku form, 10" x 8".

Robert Piepenburg, raku form with two infolding intestinal like areas in the wall, 14" high.

Robert Piepenburg, raku form with an invaginated top, 11" high.

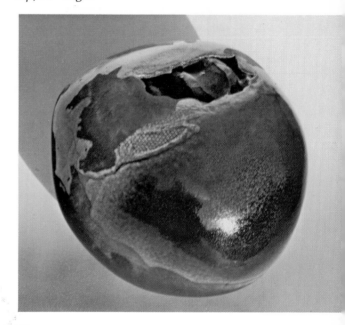

*huck Sharbaugh (student), ceramic form, 18" across. The *dy is raku fired: unglazed with a heavy smoke reduc-*n. The tongue-like part is bisque-fired clay with a pink *oxy resin coating. The resin (DER-331) and the curing *ent (DEH-14) along with the pink colorant that was *dded to the mixture are from the Dow Chemical Company.

Ken Hendry, raku pot 12" high. The simple and unassuming top is in keeping with nature and raku.

bowls are undulating so that the rims feel pleasant to the lips when the bowls are held to the mouth. The base of the bowls are usually left unglazed exposing the clay from which the bowl was made. The only decoration, except for the soft thick glaze, is the interplay of the natural colors and contours. The shapes of raku tea bowls are infinite. The shorter, flatter bowls with large surface diameters cool the tea and are used in the summer; the taller bowls with smaller rim diameters are usually used in the winter to retard the rapid cooling of the tea.

Hand-made raku bowls are often formed from a lump of clay that is pushed, pulled, and worked by the fingers into a crude-looking mug shape. When leather hard, the form is then held upside down, and a footrim is

The Saihoji garden, or moss garden, located in the western part of Kyoto. It dates back to the fourteenth century.

Nancy Jurs, multi-colored hinged raku box, 4" x 15".

Black raku tea bowl named Tamamushi, *"Golden Beetle"; bears the seal of Donyu, the most famous member of the Raku family (early Edo period). It is 3⅜" high and 5" in diameter.*

carved from the thick base with a bamboo knife. The carving is done by using as few knife strokes as possible; the footrim is often made from only one stroke of the knife. It is the aim of the potter to put the essence of his entire being into the forming of the foot. The knife marks and the foot are prized because it is said that the maker of the bowl can be understood through these marks.

A Short History

No one knows exactly how and where the use of lead glazes and tongs first developed in the firing of raku. Lead glazes were used in Egypt and Persia as long ago as 500 B.C. In Japan, low-fired earthenware with lead glaze was made in the government kilns at Nara for use in the imperial court in the seventh century A.D. It is not known if tongs were used for removing this ceramic ware from the kiln. In form and color the green-and-white lead-glazed Nara ware resembled the ware of the Chinese T'ang Dynasty, and pieces were frequently mistaken for Chinese imports. In the twelfth century the use of lead glazes had disappeared in Japan and they did not reappear until the sixteenth century.

Historical Periods Relevant to the Study of Eastern Ceramics

Japanese	Chinese
Nara (645–794 A.D.)	T'ang Dynasty (618–908 A.D.)
Heian (794–1185 A.D.)	Sung Dynasty (960–1127 A.D.)
Kamakura (1185–1392 A.D.)	
Early Muromachi (1392–1395 A.D.)	Ming Dynasty (1369–1644 A.D.)
Late Muromachi (1395–1573 A.D.)	
Momoyama (1573–1614 A.D.)	
Edo (1614–1868 A.D.)	
Meiji (1868–1920 A.D.)	

Because the Japanese government did not adopt the Western calendar until after the Meiji era, some discrepancies exist between the Western and early Japanese lunar calendar. China did not adopt the Gregorian calendar until the year 1912.

John Loree, altered wheel-thrown raku bottles;
left, 7¼″ x 15″; right, 7½″ x 10″.

John Loree, wheel-thrown raku bottle with brushed slip decoration, 5½″ x 14″.

The history of pottery in Japan is obscure. Ceramics was a local enterprise and there are no written records and few artifacts. Japan, like many countries of the east, went through periods of centralized authority and through periods of feudal rule. The Nara period and the later Heian period were times of central imperial power, and there was much Chinese influence and a lively commercial exchange between Japan and China.

During the Heian period, the central government began to crumble and the ruling power in Japan passed from the regency of the imperial family to a military government whose capital was in Kamakura. During the feudal Kamakura period loyalty and obligations of the local lords were linked to military strongmen. In this respect the period was somewhat comparable to that of Europe during the Middle Ages. Barons and lords held territory but were forced to pay tribute to military overlords (shogun) and the emperor, who was even more remote. A system of checks and balances maintained some stability and control over military conflict. However, Japan was not a unified country—it was a group of small principalities held together by military and political alliances.

During the Heian period (794–1185 A.D.), there was little progress in Japanese ceramics. Official relations with China were severed and the knowledge of Chinese pottery and glazes was lost. This was tragic since some of the loveliest pieces of Chinese ceramics were produced during this period. Porcelain was developed at this time by the Chinese, although it did not reach its zenith until the Ming Dynasty. Japanese ceramics declined, and lacquerware became popular. The Japanese almost lost interest in ceramics. The widespread popularity and use of lacquer is frequently given as a reason for the late development of their pottery.

The Japanese aristocracy of the Kamakura and Muromachi periods between the twelfth and the sixteenth centuries were importing ceramics of the Sung Dynasty, and the Sung influence can be seen on the Seto ware of that time. The real influence of the Chinese on the growth of native Japanese ceramics did not occur until about the fifteenth century when official trade was reopened with Ming China, and large quantities of Chinese ceramics were imported. This pottery was immediately prized by the feudal and military lords and appreciation of ceramics reached a new level. The introduction of Chinese ceramics was such a stimulus to the Japanese that by the end of the Muromachi period the products of several Japanese kilns were beginning to reflect a new energy and a vigorous new growth; at the same time Chinese pottery and ceramic ware had reached its last flowering.

Bill Stewart, Kangaroo Urn, *a raku pot with inlaid designs and cast forms, 24" high.*

Zen Buddhism and the Tea Ceremony

During the Muromachi period, pottery was not the only Chinese art that was popular and appreciated in Japan. The drinking of tea, which was closely associated with Zen Buddhism, developed into a ceremony and led to new vistas of human consciousness and expression—particularly in pottery.

In seeking these new vistas, we must remember that each of us is a special being with a unique spirit. If we are not alert to ourselves we will be unable to realize the spirit that is in each of us and we will be unable to accept the spirit and meanings of raku. The tea ceremony with the help of raku tea bowls was used to span the gap between spirit and embodiment in Japan.

Buddhism originated in India during the sixth century B.C. It later emerged in China and was adopted in Japan. Buddhism reached great heights in India during the third century A.D.; it later died out in India, but it had been brought to Ceylon, Burma, Tibet, China, and Japan. Various sects and movements have emerged from Buddhism. Zen Buddhism, one of these sects, became very active and strong in Japan.

As early as the Nara period (645–794 A.D.), the Japanese were importing tea from China. In the year 729, Emperor Shōmu Tenno ceremonially served powdered tea at his palace to over one hundred Buddhist monks after they had chanted the Sutras. One of the monks is said to have gone on and built forty temples, each with tea shrubs in its gardens. Later, in 1191 A.D., a monk brought Sung tea seeds from China and planted them near Kyoto, in the Uji district. Tea that was cultivated in Uji was used for ceremonial purposes and it is still thought by many to be the best tea in the world.

By the end of the fourteenth century, tea drinking had spread from the Zen monasteries to the aristocracy where tea identification contests were held. Prizes were given for correctly identifying the types of leaves used and the districts from which the leaves originated. The prizes were often lavish—a house and servants for life. Two hundred years later, owing to the patronage of the shogun Ashikaga Yoshimasa, tea drinking became an independent and secular ceremony. During this time, emphasis

Bruce Brown (student), freely built raku slab platter, 20" wide.

was placed on the beauty and rareness of the tea vessels, the skill of the brewers, and the decor of the tearooms.

Marata Shuko (1422–1503 A.D.) is considered the founder of the Japanese tea ceremony; he established a new philosophy for the drinking of tea. This philosophy was based on spiritual accord. Shuko sought a spiritual relationship between host and guest. Rank and status were forgotten during the ritual of the tea ceremony.

When Shuko was a young priest he was asked to leave the temple because he kept falling asleep. A doctor prescribed tea as a stimulant for him, and he began drinking tea and serving it to his friends. When the shogun, Yoshimasa, heard of this, he ordered Shuko to arrange a ceremony for the drinking of tea. Although special etiquette was already in use, Shuko set new rules for tea drinking and organized the formal tea ceremony. He became the first Tea Master in Japan. Shuko devoted himself to the art of drinking and serving tea, and tea flourished. Jo-o, a disciple of

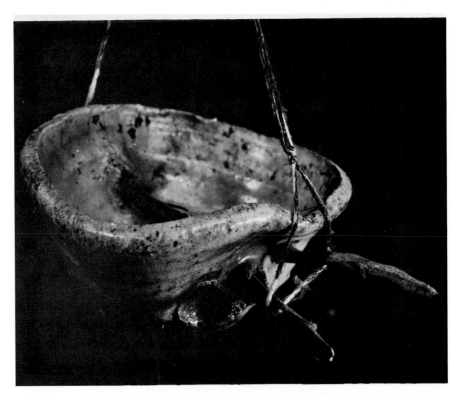

Angelo C. Garzio, raku bird feeder, 8″ wide and 5″ deep. The wheel-thrown pot was deformed and pierced to receive two branches for hanging.

Shuko, further developed Shuko's theories by introducing the concept of *wabi* which can be best described as the avoidance of luxury and falsity. Jo-o felt that human vanity must be absent from the tea ceremony. He relied on austere and simple analogies from nature to define this frame of mind.

Wabi

Sen-no Rikyu (1521–1591 A.D.), a disciple and student of Jo-o, perfected the philosophy of tea and carried it to its zenith. Rikyu is considered Japan's greatest Tea Master. As a close friend and retainer of Toyotomi Hideyoshi, the shogun, or supreme commander, of the army of Japan, Rikyu reformed the rules of the tea ceremony completing its Japanization to suit the ordinary people and surroundings of Japan.

Wabi is the natural expression of feelings that are neither ostentatious nor imposing, and its spirit is the essence of the tea ceremony. A Buddhist might use the word *compassion* to describe the feeling of the ritual; an occidental might use the word *love*. It is that part of our being which emanates a simple and open love and an honest experience of union— whether it is the love of another human being or the empathy for leaves floating in the wind. The following is a selection of verses written by Rikyu explaining the meaning of *wabi* and the spirit of the tea ceremony:

Many though there be
Who with words or even hands
Know the Way of Tea.
Few there are or none at all,
Who can serve it from the heart.

If you have one pot
And can make your tea in it
That will do quite well.
How much does he lack himself
Who must have a lot of things.

When you hear the splash
Of the water drops that fall
Into the stone bowl
You will feel that all the dust
Of your mind is washed away.

In my little hut,
Whether people come or not
It is all the same.
In my heart there is no stir.
Of attraction or disgust.

There is no fixed rule
As to when the window should
Closed or open be.
It depends on how the moon
Or the snow their shadows cast.

Flowers of hill or dale
Put them in a simple vase
Full or brimming o'er.
But when you're arranging them
You must slip your heart in too.

Though invisible
There's a thing that should be swept
With our busy broom.
'Tis the dirt that ever clings
To the impure human heart.

Though you wipe your hands
And brush off the dust and dirt
From the tea vessels.
What's the use of all this fuss
If the heart is still impure?

When you take a sip
From the bowl of powder tea
There within it lies
Clear reflected in its depths
Blue of sky and gray of sea.

In the Dewy Path
And the tearoom's calm retreat
Host and guests have met.
Not an inharmonious note
Should disturb their quiet zest.

The rigid rules of the tea ceremony were to have a profound influence on Japanese art and the conduct of everyday life. The influence of the Tea Masters gave emphasis to the beauty of humility and the love of simplicity. Through their teachings, the spirit of the tea ceremony was to enter every aspect of Japanese life and culture. The popularity of the tea ceremony during the Momoyama period (1573–1614 A.D.) was responsible for the

Paul Soldner, unglazed and heavily smoked wheel-thrown pot, 12″ high. The white slip decorations with iron and copper are glazed finger and palm prints.

appreciation and development of ceramics, particularly the ware used for the drinking of tea. Many types of ceremonial pottery were valued, each for its distinctive beauty, and each reflecting the Tea Master's philosophy and taste.

The Raku Family

If you study tea ware, you might encounter some of the following names:

Chien Yao or *Temmoku,* Sung Dynasty, 960–1127 A.D.

Raku, favored by Sen-no Rikyu, 1521–1591 A.D

Asahi, one of the seven famous kilns of the tea master Kobori Enshu, 1579–1647 A.D.

Shino, Seto wares favored by the tea master Shino Soshin.

Oribe, wares made in Narumi for the tea master Furuta Oribe, 1544–1615 A.D.

Karatsu, Korean styled wares from the island of Kyushu, highly influenced by the Korean Yi Dynasty, 1392–1900 A.D.

There are many other names that could be included, these are listed simply to show that *Rakuyaki*—the raku bowl—was not the only kind of ware used in the tea ceremonies. Raku bowls, however, were favored by most connoisseurs. Besides being pleasing to the touch, and possessing that wonderful feeling of tranquility characteristic of *wabi,* the tea seemed to taste better in raku bowls. When the quality of water used for making tea was to be judged, or tested, the water was tasted from the raku tea bowl. Also, the highly grogged and porous clay body used for raku made an excellent insulated container for hot tea.

Although raku ware was guided to fame in Kyoto by Sen-no Rikyu —because it was favored by him for use in the tea ceremony—the raku ware itself was originated by Chojiro, the son of a Korean tile maker. During the 1520s Chojiro settled in Kyoto, and took the title Sokei after marrying into a Japanese family, and became naturalized. Rikyu became so fond of Chojiro that he honored him by giving him his father's name of Tanaka.

Paul Soldner, altered wheel-thrown pot, 16" high. Partly glazed with iron and copper over a white slip.

The designs of Chojiro's soft earthenware reflected the wide bottom style of Korean tea bowls. His wares were usually glazed with one of two colors, and raku is still classified as either black or red raku ware. Chojiro's glazes were of the soft lead type, resembling those produced in the Chinese T'ang and Ming Dynasties.

The black glaze Chojiro developed is said to have two parts Kamogawa stone, mined from the Kamo River, to one part Japanese frit, made from ground lead glass. Kamogawa stone, or black stone, is similar in composition to barnard clay, with the same proportions of alumina, silica, and iron. Before glazing, the ware was bisqued to a bright cherry-red or orange at a temperature of about 1600° F. (If the bisque temperature were carried any higher the ware would become very vitreous and develop a harsh sounding ping when tapped by a fingernail or brushed as the tea was being stirred. The tea master, no doubt, would find such sounds disturbing to the serenity and peaceful atmosphere of the tea house.)

The red raku ware that is made in Japan today is said to be covered with a yellow-ochre slip prior to bisquing. Some red raku tea bowls have dark, smoky areas created by trapped carbon. These areas can be artificially induced by a special firing following the bisque firing. This is done by placing the ochre bowls in a box of burning charcoal and then dipping them in water to cool. Afterwards, a transparent lead glaze is applied by either brushing or dipping.

It is not known if a similar formula was used by Chojiro. He might have used a lead and Japanese frit glaze over a reddish clay body, or he may have used a glaze of almost one quarter red iron oxide and even twice as much ochre. Reds are difficult to achieve and they are usually made in a muffle (a protective fireclay box within the kiln) and fired at temperatures well below the 1600° F. usually used for bisquing or the higher glaze temperatures used for black raku. Chojiro probably glaze-fired his raku ware in a wood-burning muffle kiln, and watched the firing through a hole in the lid. The correct temperature was determined by the color of the ware and the kiln's interior, or by the removal of glazed draw rings. At the correct temperature the ware—especially if it were glazed black—would be removed from the hot kiln with long-handled tongs, and immersed in a concentrated solution of green tea. Not all ware is quenched in a tea solution; some ware is removed from the kiln and placed directly on cool bricks or tiles and allowed to oxidize. But, the soft and subtle crackling or crazing of the glaze can best be achieved by allowing the ware to oxidize a few seconds before it is quenched.

Among the tea bowls that Chojiro made, seven became very famous:

Robert Piepenburg, multi-glazed wheel-thrown raku bottle, 12½" high.

Robert Piepenburg, Global Village, *multi-glazed raku form, 15" high.*

One of Chojiro's bowls is called *Daikoku*, The Great Black. It is a little over three inches high and no more than four inches in diameter. It was admired for its rustic and quiet appearance, and was one of Rikyu's most cherished possessions.

Another, called *Toyobo*, was given to the Toyobo Hall at the Shinnyodo Temple by Rikyu. Both bowls are owned by the Konoike family of Osaka and are considered to be in accord with the spirit of *wabi*.

Two more of the famous seven are named *Kengyo* and *Komori*, because they were not appreciated by the connoisseurs. Once, when Rikyu went to Chojiro for tea bowls, the potter had only one. He told Rikyu that the reason he had that one bowl was that, like the blind minstrel, no one wanted it; that bowl was named *Kengyo*. *Komori* is the name given to the last piece of fruit left on a tree as a "guard" during the winter. Rikyu asked his pupils to select the bowls they liked best. One of the ten bowls that he showed them was not chosen by any of the pupils. Rikyu purposely called it *Komori*.

The fifth bowl was named *Hayabune*, meaning swift ship, because Rikyu had a swift ship sent from Kyoto to Korea to bring the bowl for use in serving tea.

The sixth bowl Rikyu named *Rinzai*, because it possessed the preeminence of the great Zen monk *Rinzai*.

The last of Chojiro's seven famous bowls is called the *Hachibiraki*, the Inauguration bowl, because Rikyu had planned to use it for the first time in serving tea to a powerful shogun.

The name raku comes from a gold seal granted to Chojiro's younger brother, Jokei, by the shogun Hideyoshi. Until that time, the ware was called "now ware" or "Kyoto ware." It was six years after Chojiro's death when the honor was bestowed. The gold seal was given in memory of Chojiro and bore the ideograph *raku*, a symbol that, freely translated, means enjoyment, contentment, pleasure, and happiness. The written character for the word raku comes from Hideyoshi's pleasure pavilion in Kyoto named Ju-raku-tei; Chojiro and his brother had made roof tiles for this pavilion. The surviving brother adopted and used Raku as a family name. From that time on, the Raku family tradition continued—and continues today.

Robert Piepenburg, paddled wheel made vase with a congenial slab top, 11" high.

Following is a list of the generations of the house of Raku:

THIRD GENERATION:	Donyu, the son of Jokei. Died 1656.
FOURTH GENERATION:	Ichinyu, the son of Donyu. Died 1682.
FIFTH GENERATION:	Sonyu, a pupil of Ichinyu. Died 1725.
SIXTH GENERATION:	Sanyu, the adopted son of Sonyu. Died 1740.
SEVENTH GENERATION:	Chonyu, Sanyu's younger brother. Died 1769.
EIGHTH GENERATION:	Tokunyu, Chonyu's adopted son. Died 1775.
NINTH GENERATION:	Ryonyu, Tokunyu's son. Died 1835.
TENTH GENERATION:	Tannyu, the son of Ryonyu. Died 1854.
ELEVENTH GENERATION:	Keinyu, Tannyu's son. Died 1893.
TWELFTH GENERATION:	Kichizayemon.
THIRTEENTH GENERATION:	Ryonyu.
FOURTEENTH GENERATION:	Kichizayemon.

Tea Masters and Potters

Ogata Kenzan (1661–1742 A.D.) was one of Japan's greatest potters and also one of the world's great artists. Besides being acclaimed for his painting and poetry, he was a famous Tea Master. This title and honor was granted only to a true artist who had sufficient awareness and insight into nature and man. There were other famous potters who were also tea masters, but many potters were overshadowed by the Tea Masters for whom they made tea bowls. Although Chojiro was the potter who originated the ware, it is often—even now—referred to as "Rikyu ware," not because it was made by Rikyu, but because Rikyu was Japan's most famous Tea Master and raku ware was prized and made famous by him.

Little would be known of raku pottery in today's Western world had it not been for Bernard Leach. Leach, an Englishman, studied pottery in Japan with a sixth generation representative of Ogata Kenzan. Between 1911 and 1920, with the exceptions of the years 1915 through 1917 which he spent in China, Leach made raku pottery in Tokyo. He became a seventh generation representative of the Kenzan tradition, with certification from his master, and continued to produce raku pottery in England between 1920 and 1930. His book, *A Potter's Book*, published in 1940, is credited with introducing and describing raku pottery outside of Japan.

Warren Gilbertson is probably the first American to introduce raku ware to this country. After Gilbertson returned from Japan, he exhibited over 250 pieces of pottery at the Art Institute of Chicago. It was during this exhibit, in November and December of 1941, that a number of raku pieces were shown. The simple techniques used in raku attracted some American potters in the early 1950s, but raku was not pursued seriously in the United States until the 1960s.

Paul Soldner is most responsible for the direction and popularity of raku in this country. In 1960 Soldner started making post fired reduction raku pottery in Los Angeles, California. Many of his pieces are wheel-thrown bulbous forms that have been altered by the addition of clay and other surface treatments. They often reflect an elusive, subtle, yet vigorous beauty. Soldner's works and those of many other contemporaries, some-how manage to perpetuate the fundamental and universal rhythms of life associated with raku pottery.

Whether or not today's raku potter should reflect the philosophical Oriental heritage in his ceramic forms is a matter of personal choice. If an American potter were to incorporate some other standard of form for expression, as seen in the work represented in this book, there would be no need to feel any apprehension; it is not the form or even the philosophy of raku that is important—the form will disappear in time, it is sure to be broken—it is the experience that lives and moves life forward.

2
The Ceremony of Tea,
Cha-No-Yu

The Tea Ceremony, like raku, is almost synonomous with Japan. For centuries the tea ceremony, called *Cha-No-Yu* (hot water for tea), has been responsible for creating an appreciation and understanding of raku pottery. The tea ceremony used raku tea bowls because they symbolized the beauty, the simple and unassuming qualities, that were in harmony with everyday life.

The Japanese use the word *Shibui* to express this quality of beauty: a beauty that might be associated with humility, unpretentious virtue, and unassuming tastefulness. Because of its manifold relationships with philosophy and religion and its emphasis on simplicity and natural beauty, a knowledge of the tea ceremony is helpful in understanding and appreciating its influence both in the field of ceramics and on the conduct of life. Understanding this quality of beauty sets the mood for the making of raku pottery much in the same way a tea garden is used to set the mood for the tea ceremony.

Though the ceremony itself contains a mixture of the ancient cultures of India and China, it was the Japanese spirit that transformed and adapted the ceremony into the epitome of Japanese institutions and civilization. The ceremony derives its origin from Chinese Zen Buddhism and the elaborate ritual of drinking tea before the image of Bodhidharma, the semi-legendary

Raku Tea Bowl bearing the mark of Jokei.

figure of the first patriarch of Chinese Zen. Perhaps the greatest contribution made by Zen to the secularization of the Japanese ceremony of tea was the concept of equal importance: the littleness of greatness and the greatness of littleness in all things. The whole ideal behind the ceremonial form of tea drinking is the Zen concept of no distinction of importance between incidents of life.

There are almost as many approaches to the tea ceremony as there are tea masters, but they differ little in the essentials. There are three distinct phases in the ceremony: a meal called *Kaiseki* is the first phase; the second is *Koicha* or the thick-tea phase; and the third, the thin-tea phase, is known as *Usu-Cha.* Any one, or all three phases, may be chosen and served by the host.

The *Usu-Cha* phase is the most popular and usually the only one served because it takes three to four hours (which includes recesses spent in the garden) in order to properly serve all three. The ceremony in its entirety is usually reserved for special occasions, such as the celebration of a birth, or those special occasions or holidays for which a Westerner might give a dinner party.

To insure an atmosphere of quiet serenity and isolation from worldly distractions, an elaborate code of etiquette and rules govern the ritual and the conduct of the participants. These rules demand strict observance. The practices, many of which were instituted by Rikyu, begin with the host extending the invitation days in advance to not more than five, but not

less than three, guests. Frequently, there is a guest of honor or number one guest, for whom the ceremony is given. The day before the ceremony the guests call on the host to express their thanks in advance. The day of the ceremony the host is busy with elaborate preparations: cleaning the tearoom, privy, and garden; selecting the utensils and alcove decoration; and planning the food.

The Day of the Ceremony

The guests arrive early to change footwear and, perhaps, some clothing. They assemble in a portico located in the outer garden which also contains the waiting arbor and the privy. Here they are to admire the garden and, in effect, shed their worldly cares. If no guest of honor has been chosen by the host, the guests will now decide who will be "guest number one": the guest whose lead the others will follow in a predetermined manner from the outer garden through the middle gate and into the inner garden.

When the host is ready the guests are summoned to the tearoom by way of the garden path connecting the teahouse and the portico. The walk on the path is intended to remove the thoughts and spirit of the outside world and to produce a quiet and tranquil mood that will be conducive to the serenity of the tearoom. The intended sensation of the walk varies. Some tea masters aim at purity of spirit, others seek solitude, while some—like Rikyu—sought to achieve loneliness. The ingenuity involved in the planning and preparation of the garden has much to do with a particular effect. Stepping stones, chosen for their irregularity are arranged with scrupulous care; a quiet rock-lined pond might be placed where it will reflect an autumn moon; an earthen bridge could pass fragrant pines and lead to a hill of maple trees containing a moss-covered stone lantern. Although the garden path would have been cleaned only hours before the ceremony, the host will often take great pains to produce an effect of the rustic naturalness by the studied placement of dried pine

A totally serene view of the pathway approaching a teahouse in Kyoto. Note the stone washbasin in the center foreground.

Japanese teahouse and garden at Sambo-in (near Kyoto) used by Hideyoshi.

needles or by the careful shaking of a tree limb so that the loosened leaves might add their natural beauty to the path. As they silently approach the teahouse, the guests pause just outside the tearoom at a special stone washbasin filled with peaceful sounding trickles of running water. With a dipper, they perform a formal purification of the rinsing of the hands and mouth, and then pass directly into the tearoom.

The opening to the tearoom through which they pass is quite small. It is a standard twenty-seven inches by thirty-six inches, a size originally decided by Rikyu, causing each guest to enter by bending in a manner symbolic of humility. One by one the guests noiselessly pass from the vexations of the world outside and enter, in an order of precedence formerly agreed upon, into the sanctuary of the tearoom. Prior to seating, the guests stop to admire the painted calligraphy on a scroll in the alcove, which is a replica of the altar in Zen chapels, and perhaps the tiny incense holder and the raku or porcelain water jar.

David Keyes, raku plate, 13" x 14".

Bamboo water dipper, 16¼" long.

When the guests are silently seated and there is no sound but the bubbling of water boiling in the iron kettle, which is heated by a seventeen-inch-square sunken fire box called the *Ro,* the host will make his appearance. In the summer, or when there is no hearth, a three-footed furnace is used and a trivet is placed in the inside bottom to support the kettle.

The host does not enter from the guest doorway but through another entrance adjoining a pantry where the utensils are cleaned and arranged. After bowing and greeting his guests, the host sits with his body at a forty-five-degree angle to the hearth, facing his guest of honor with whom he will speak mostly.

In a short time the host will serve the *Kaiseki,* a simple but excellent meal, that has been prepared with the utmost care. The meal might consist of no more than soup and cakes, or it might include pickles, broiled fish, roasted chestnuts, vegetables, mushrooms, and seaweed. It is not customary for the host to eat with his guests. The host serves every dish himself, so that the tranquil atmosphere is not disturbed by the intrusion of servants.

Afterwards, there may be ceremonious drinking of saki, followed by the serving of sweets. Then there is the ceremonial cleaning of the fingers and lips with salt or herb flavored warm water. The guests will then take a recess in the garden to chat and await the sounding of the ceremonial gong to signal their return to the tearoom and the ritual serving of tea.

Serving the Tea

Upon their return to the tearoom, the guests may find the scroll in the alcove replaced with a simple flower arrangement. After the prescribed acts of etiquette have been completed the *Koicha* or thick-tea is ready to be served. It is prepared from leaves of the highest quality that have been especially harvested and processed for the tea rites. Two or three spoonfuls of the powdered tea are removed from the thick-tea caddy and put into a tea bowl. The bowl may or may not be raku, depending upon the personal taste of the host, or the school of tea with which he is associated. A special spoon is used for transferring the powdered tea; it is usually hand-carved bamboo, and made by the host. Hot water, taken from the kettle with a bamboo dipper, is poured into the bowl and the tea beaten with a bamboo whisk to a frothy soup resembling "liquid jade." The whisk, split into threads at one end and conforming to the bottom contour of the bowl, makes a soft, rushing sound, far more pleasing than the sound made by a metal implement.

In turn, each guest drinks a portion of the tea: After first admiring the bowl they will take one sip; compliment the host on its flavor; noisily take two or three more sips; and then pass the bowl on until each guest has tasted the tea. Protocol demands that each guest wipe the part of the bowl touched by his lips with a small white paper before passing it. When the bowl has been returned to the host, the guest of honor may ask that

The guest of honor goes first to the alcove to admire the painting and flower arrangement.

The host uses the dipper to transfer the hot water from the kettle to the tea bowl. Note the use of the stand or daisu *for holding tea utensils at a formal serving.*

the bowl be passed again to allow for closer inspection and appreciation of its qualities. The spoon and tea caddy may also be circulated for appreciation. A small silk square is often used by the guests when handling the tea utensils. This ends the second phase of the ceremony.

Although two or three hours have passed since the ceremony began, the guests are neither bored nor tired, because they were carefully selected by the host for their congeniality. The third or final phase is marked by the serving of the thin tea. The thin tea, served at this less formal yet most often used third sitting, is inferior to the thick tea. The tea is removed from the thin-tea caddy, and prepared in a similar manner. The general difference is that each guest empties the tea bowl, wipes the rim with his fingers, wipes his fingers with a small white paper, and then returns the bowl directly to the host. The host washes it out with hot water, empties the water into the waste-water holder, wipes it with a small linen cloth, and brews new tea in the bowl for the next guest. The bowl is then presented best side forward to the guest. The guest, with careful and precise movements, turns it in his hands so that he does not sip from the best side. A sweet jelly confection is also served at this time.

With departing salutations the guests take their leave. They return, as etiquette demands, on the following day to convey their appreciation and thanks for the host's kindness. If the guest of honor is of exceptionally high rank the host may escort him part of the way home and call on him the following day to once again thank him for coming.

Teaism

Japanese civilization might be referred to as a tea civilization. By Western standards, the tea ceremony is not religious but rather a social institution. Its manifestations might be better understood if the tea rites are compared to some of the practices of Western religions; the similarities are many. Parishioners arrive at the church (tearoom) before the service (ceremony), sit quietly (meditate), and wait for the entrance of the priest (host). The altar (alcove) will display a symbolic cloth covering (scroll) and perhaps an arrangement of flowers. The priest (host) upon entering will symbolically greet his congregation (guests). In many churches Holy Communion will be the climax of the service (ceremony) with the serving

Raku tea bowl, middle Edo period.

Bamboo tea wisk (4¼" high) and spoon (7¼" long). The tea bowl is an early work of Rev. N. S. Kobori (Daitokuji, Kyoto, Japan) and is owned by Sandor B. Brent.

and receiving of the bread (confection) and the wine (tea). Other parallels exist in the way the sections of the ceremony are cherished by the participants.

Religious artifacts are often exceedingly ornate and frequently valued as much for their luxurious appearance as for their religious antiquity and association. I have heard of some raku tea bowls belonging to great tea masters valued at over $100,000 because of the personal association. However, raku tea bowls, in addition to their associative value, are adored for their simple naturalness and avoidance of luxury.

The architecture and interiors of churches and the architecture and interiors of teahouses, are also fundamentally similar in purpose; they are both designed and consecrated for a specific ceremony.

Early tearooms, and many modern ones, are simply areas in the home partitioned off from other areas with screens. The tearoom, whether it is part of the house or a separate teahouse, is used only for ceremonial purposes. The proportions of the room vary. In Japan the woven mats called *tatami* are an architectural standard of measurement—*tatami* are three feet by six feet by one-and-one-half-inch thick rough straw mattresses with a finely woven straw cover. Tea ceremony rooms are usually anywhere from two to four and one-half mats in area. The popular size is four and one-half mats.

A. Stepping Stones
B. Guest Entrance (Nijiriguchi)
C. Guests' Mat (Kyaku-Datami)
D. Guest of Honor's Mat (Kinin-Datami)
E. Alcove (Tokonoma)
F. Utensil Mat (Dogu-Datami)
G. Hearth Mat (Ro)
H. Hearth Half Mat (Ro-Datami)
I. Host's Entry Mat (Fungomi-Datami)
J. Host's Entrance (Sadoguchi)
K. Host (Teishu)
L. Guest of Honor (Shokyaku)
M.-P. Guests (Kyaku)

Rikyu's Design for a 4½ Mat Tearoom

Rikyu's Design for a 2 Mat Tearoom

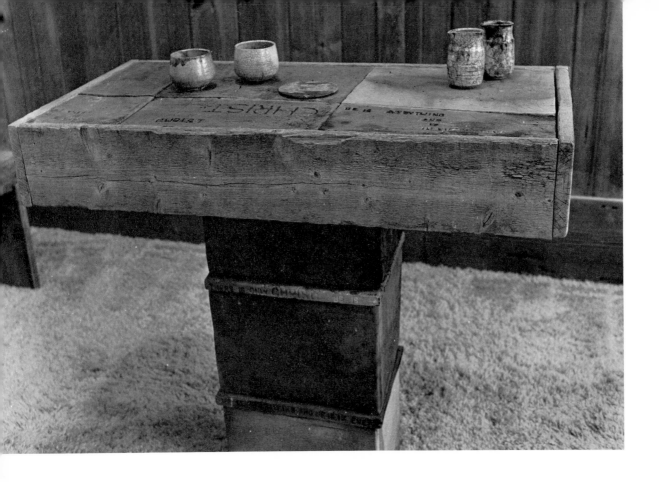

Top, *Sister Celeste Mary Bourke, raku altar and appointments in a small chapel at Siena Heights College. The three supporting boxes and altar top are smoked clay only. Bottom, The candle holders, cruets, chalices, and tabernacle, which opens at the top, are covered with a transparent glaze.*

*George Timock, red and black
raku slab construction, 16½″ x 45″.*

Bruce Brown (student), hand-built raku bowl with negative areas and pinched foot, 4½" x 7".

Teahouses built in the traditional style reflect a deliberate form of architectural purity that is unprepossessing. Although they resemble nothing more than a straw-covered hut with mud-covered walls, they are made from the finest materials and with meticulous care, and often cost as much as the main house. The secret of the tearoom lies in its undecorated walls and its simple unadorned beauty. There are no distractions. The room is calm, and its ambience does not distract the mind, but rather, frees the participant to become aware of and recognize the beauty of other things. It is often said that the tearoom draws out the beauty of the utensils.

Architecturally Rikyu revolutionized tearoom design. Using the standard four-and-one-half-mat floor plan established by Jo-o, Rikyu did away with Jo-o's open veranda design which made the garden and room's interior a single space. With the exception of a few small windows, the tearoom was to become a cosmos in itself—independent in architectural style and independent of the outside world. Searching for structural purity Rikyu substituted natural log posts for the planed and square supports. Ornaments and decorated door panels were eliminated, and the walls were made of clay similar to the clay used for the walls of simple farmhouses.

Rikyu did not recognize social rank in the tearoom and insisted that men of different status forget their distinctions and aim for spiritual accord. To encourage deeper spiritual accord, Rikyu reduced the floor area from four and one-half tatami mats (the minimum space necessary to prevent an aristocrat from bumping knees with someone of lesser station) to two mats. It was such disregard for rank and station that angered Rikyu's fierce

Mary Whiteford (student), slab built weed holder, 9" high.

patron, Hideyoshi, who eventually condemned Rikyu to die, with honor, by Rikyu's own hand.

Tearooms and the tea ceremony, like Japan itself, have undergone many changes since the time of Rikyu and Chojiro. Traditionally, tea encompassed the culture and all the art forms that are Japan. To ask to what extent a role it plays in Japanese art and life today is to ask what it exemplifies to each individual. To some it might mean little compared to the universal trends and intrusions that accompany expanding technologies. It is, however, improbable for the spirit of tea not to exist somewhere within, hopefully seeking expression. The spirit of tea is like the spirit of life. To ask contemporary raku potters to concern themselves with it might be too much, yet it lingers deep in the nativity of raku pottery. To envision its latent potential to affect our work and lives, one must come face to face with its meaning. To understand the spirit of tea is to delve into the mystery of ourselves and the metamorphosis implicit in clay.

> *Be prepared for the moment*
> *For we were once a moment*
> *Becoming a moment*
> *To become a moment*
> *To become a moment*
> *To become*
> *To be.*
>
> RON ALDRICH

> *I embrace this man of clay with holiness*
> *This man, who sows the seed, the holy clay*
> *From which the seeds of life are growing*
> *Earth of hope and nourishment*
> *Perpetually erupting in forms of love.*
> *Deeply, he is the*
> *Earth of first beginnings, of all the aging times*
> *The fired masterpiece of all these burning cosmos.*
>
> JUDY PIEPENBURG

Gallery

Right, *Mary Town (student), hand built raku pitcher with cork, 7" high.*

Below, *Michael DelFavero (student), slab built raku form with thrown foot, 15" high.*

Opposite page, *David Middlebrook, reducing in place on the roll-out floor of the kiln by placing a metal barrel, filled with straw, over the raku form. Large pieces are fired to maturity in from six to eight hours and smoked while cooling for two to three hours in the barrel.*

David Middlebrook, Just Before Temptation, *4½' high.*

Mary Town (student), hand built raku mirror frame, 12" high. The mirror is not so much for looking into as for reflecting forms, in this case the flat coils.

Wayne Higby, The First Waterfall, *20½″ high. A landscape box with gold sun, brown cliffs, and blue and white water.*

Wayne Higby, Landscape Storage Jar, *11-13" x 13". Reduced for several hours in wet straw.*

Ruth Ellen Hollingsworth, Alice's Rocker, *13" x 13" x 31". The piece was made in two sections and assembled after the firing. It is fitted with a macrame seat cushion and arm covers.*

3

Clay: Material and Medium

Raku pottery is earth derived. Clay has little value in itself; any value it may have is based upon man and his relationship to the clay.

The raku tea bowl is more than a receptacle for tea; it carries human sensory experience. Clay is more than a material, it is a medium for unlimited form and expression. It can, without the use of any tool—except the miracle of man's hands—be made to bear forth, incarnate, our sense of life. As reasoning beings we are sometimes aware of the unity between clay and man; but when we function as potters, we often become completely involved in production and the technical process of the work— sometimes to the exclusion of everything else. Although in this chapter we will discuss clay in the material-technical sense, a potter should always remember that potting—like life—is not a technical process. A few potters approach clay as a scientific exercise, but most learn about and become involved with the technical aspects only when this knowledge is needed.

Tom Johns (student), raku bowl made from a porcelain clay body containing neither sand nor grog, 5" wide. It was included in the first firing of a cold raku kiln and fired to maturity within an hour.

To make good pottery there must be a feeling for clay. Become involved with your material, get to know as much as you can about clay—the chemical make-up, the mechanics of processing the clay, the techniques for forming pieces, etc.—but never become so technically oriented that you are disloyal to your senses and feelings for the clay as a medium for expression and as a material in itself.

Encountering the Medium

It is difficult to discuss pottery without including the invisible life spirit brought to the work by the potter—his mind, his imagination, his emotions, his very being. This spirit can be related to the spirit of the clay. Before telling my beginning students about the methods and procedures for forming clay, I usually conduct them through an "encounter session" with the substance itself.

As a group I invite them to dig a lump of clay from the barrel using their fingers and become acquainted with the substance by working and playing with it. In summer sessions we start by mixing the clay outdoors.

The students, in bare feet, form a tight circle. With the help of a hose and a hoe, powdered clay is trampled from a dry to a liquid to a plastic material. After the students become familiar with this initial tactile experience, more directed activities are attempted. The clay is rolled; pinched; dropped on the table; thrown on the table; pressed; twisted; tasted (chewed, not swallowed); poked; smoothed; and silently, with closed eyes, fondled. Some of the unending possibilities are explored.

Immediately following this exploratory and tactile phase, I usually ask the students to react to the clay as an artistic and creative medium. They are asked to work with the clay in the most imaginative way they can. Some students experiment with textures made by their own fingers, some use objects that are found in the studio. Another request might take them outside the studio with a lump of clay to find and bring back impressions of textures found in nature.

Next they create a rigid, structured, geometric type of form—with neat, sharp corners, made by pounding the clay on a table. They also

Students making and wedging clay with bare feet.

experiment with free-flowing organic forms by sliding the clay on the table as it is thrown. Sometimes we break up into groups of three or four and go off for fifteen minutes and make, completely through nonverbal communication, a community form. Other times the students isolate themselves for about ten minutes and create specific shapes or objects, such as a cylindrical piece so that they can experience the uniqueness of individual expression within the confines of an assigned form.

Each group of students has its own personality and, in a sense, it is this group composition that determines the direction and tempo that will be taken. It is essential that an open and running dialogue about the actions and reactions of each student is maintained. This communication helps to reveal ways in which one is prevented from feeling and experiencing the clay fully and honestly.

Each student's work is always discussed by everyone in the class before destruction—yes, destruction. One at a time the students destroy their forms and shapes, not because death is needed to bring new life, but because of the self-awareness this act inspires. Students will often slowly

Wedging clay on the studio floor. This is that shared moment when clay and potter meet and touch each other for the first time, evoking an unspoken and mysterious dialogue that ultimately unites and directs both.

Student encounter with clay. Although clay appears simple, it is limitless. Like ourselves, there are no formulas for understanding clay and working with it. The encounter is directed toward knowing, appreciating, understanding, accepting, and, most of all, letting things be what they are.

squeeze the clay between their fingers, or quietly fold the clay down on the table with the palm of their hand, they do not simply throw the clay down, as might be expected. Some students, who had wrinkled their noses as if to say "what an ugly material," when they first took the clay from the barrel, might be almost in tears when it is their turn to demolish their creation.

As a teacher of pottery, I am always trying to make the student the subject of my course—to make each student aware of himself. The "encounter with clay," that I have described, is part of the self-analysis and introspection that I believe leads to true expression. The ultimate goal is to make the material and the expression of the person, through the material, become as one. When this happens, the artist-craftsman recognizes the power and potential of the clay as a unique and universal medium and of himself as a unique creature within the universality of man.

A small group of students new to clay working together—nonverbally—to make a community form: a phase of the encounter that arouses consciousness, participation, excitement, experiences of meaning and eventually . . .

The Clay

Clay for use in raku can be found almost anywhere. The only requirements are that the clay must mature chemically at or above 1600° F.; contain enough coarse or refractory material—such as grog, sand, volcanic ash, pumice, talc, or alumina—to withstand the thermal shock; respond well to the technique of forming; and successfully survive the firing.

Clay can be used directly from the ground with no further processing. You can often find very usable clay by yourself; start your prospecting on surface outcroppings. If you want to dig and use native clays you might get some assistance in locating natural clay deposits by asking your state geologist.

Clay is basically decomposed rock. It is made by the wearing away of rocks for millions of years. Temperature, wind, water, ice, and natural plants have also served a part in the formation of clay. Look near riverbeds, dried creek beds, eroded hillsides, or any place that digging or excava-

Clay may be found near creekbeds or as surface outcroppings of the landscape.

Clay being unloaded from the mixer. For raku, the openness of clay made in a dough mixer is preferred to the dense clay from a pug mill.

tions have taken place. The quality of the clay you find can be recognized by studying the "crack patterns."

If there are deep cracks and many clear patterns are imprinted in the clay, and the clay is very "plastic," then it is probably quite pure, and not suitable for raku because it isn't porous enough. This clay might require the addition of grog or sand to increase the ability to withstand the shock of the raku firing technique and the use of tongs. If the patterns and cracks in the clay are not strongly pronounced the deposit is probably contaminated with sand or organic matter which should make it suitable for raku. If a clay source should prove to be too plastic or non-porous to survive the firing without cracking, one might add a refractory material such as sand. Experimentation might be started by firing clay containing various amounts of sand. A good starting ratio might be one part sand to two parts clay.

The processing of clay dug from a local deposit requires that it be dried and broken into small chunks prior to slaking—soaking in water till it crumbles. When it breaks up into a slip consistency, it needs only to be mixed and poured through a screen to remove any remaining lumps or stones, and placed on a plaster of paris slab to remove the excess moisture from the clay.

Many potters consider clay they have personally located and processed valuable, and generally rate their clays according to the reaction to firing. I value a clay for its working and forming properties and discovered, long ago, that the best way to obtain a clay body that is consistent and satisfactory is to blend my own instead of relying on a natural source.

The making of a workable raku clay body by blending various purchased materials is a simple procedure. A satisfactory body should contain as its main ingredient a high temperature fire clay, or bounding clay, that matures beyond 1800° F. These can be purchased from most local refractory companies and if large quantities are ordered there is quite a savings. My last order of fire clay was for one and one-half tons and the total cost was $2.50 less than the total cost of just one ton. The other basic ingredient needed is sand or grog. Grog is a refractory clay that has been fired and ground into granules. The 20-28 mesh works well. Grog is often referred to as the bones of the clay because it adds structure and lessens shrinkage during drying and thermal shock during firing. It, too, is found at most local refractory companies. Washed silica sand and beach sand in the 25-50 mesh range are excellent alternatives to grog. Not only are they half as expensive, but they adhere to the clay better. In addition, sand, unlike grog, is absorbent and clings to clay which makes it possible to create

Mark Stein (student), raku mirror frame, 15" wide. The piece was made by using a spatula to apply thick clay slip, on top of several sheets of paper much in the same way one might put frosting on a cake.

larger shapes; and when firing at the temperature necessary for raku, there is no noticeable swelling or protruding of the sand from the surface of the fired clay.

When fire clay, sand, and water are mixed in the correct proportions a satisfactory raku clay body should be the result, especially if the clay is wedged and stored for a few days before it is used. The formula for my hand-building raku clay body is as follows (by weight):

Fire clay (50 mesh*)   75%   Beach sand (45 mesh)   25%

* The mesh designation above is a measure of the particle size of the clay or sand determined by screening.

Jordan clay can be added to make the body more workable and the clay would then act as plastic low-grade fire clay. Ball clay could be substituted for Jordan at the expense of shrinkage (twenty-one percent at maturity) if greater plasticity is wanted. Most raku potters have their own clay formulas as it should be. I can only testify that mine serves me well, and has worked under many adverse conditions.

Some formulas for raku clay body contain thirty, forty, even as much as fifty percent sand or grog. Many formulas contain some ball clay, red clay, flint, and feldspar. Some bodies contain such refractories as zonolite, pearlite, and vermiculite. Most raku clay formulas consist of ten to twenty percent talc, a magnesium silicate used in the clay body to help resist shock. There is some breakage during the firing when tremoline talc has been used and so steatite talc might be substituted. I do not know what the difference is chemically, except that the tremoline talc, sometimes referred to as a calcium magnesium silicate, contains a higher percentage of calcium and less silica oxide.

Bentonite, a volcanic clay, can also be added (do not exceed two per-

Removing paper from the top of a leather-hard hanging piece, formed from a hand-thrown slab of clay rolled over the paper and bounced into shape on a table top. After glaze firing, the piece will be suspended from three holes using leather thongs.

A piece of chammy or soft leather can be used to remove the grog trails formed by wire loop trimming tools cutting through highly grogged raku clay and to smooth a trimmed foot. The potter's wheel shown was designed and is sold by Robert Piepenburg, Ann Arbor, Michigan.

cent) to make the clay more plastic. I have stopped using it because it is difficult to distribute through the body. It must be slaked in water before using, and hardly seems worth the effort. For a more plastic raku body that is suitable for work on the wheel, I use the following formula (by weight):

Jordan clay	20%
Fire clay (50 mesh)	60%
Beach sand (45 mesh)	20%

You might think that clay of a finer mesh, such as a 200 mesh air-floated fire clay, would increase plasticity, but if the 50 mesh clay is added to water and thoroughly mixed, you will be unable to tell the difference. Fire clay, regardless of its mesh, slakes down uniformly in solution. The 50 mesh, in addition to being less expensive than the smaller sized 200 mesh, is less hazardous because there is less chance of inhaling the dust and less is given off during handling and mixing. Plasticity is also increased by aging or storing the mixed clay in an airtight plastic bag or crock. Colloidal conditions that evolve through bacterial growth improve the clay's plasticity. The longer the clay is aged the better, but improvements are noticeable in two to five days.

David Middlebrook, Bubble-up, *a partially inflated latex rubber weather balloon wedged between raku fired slabs of clay, 39" wide. The piece was made by dropping wet slabs over a basketball that were then bisqued to cone 5.*

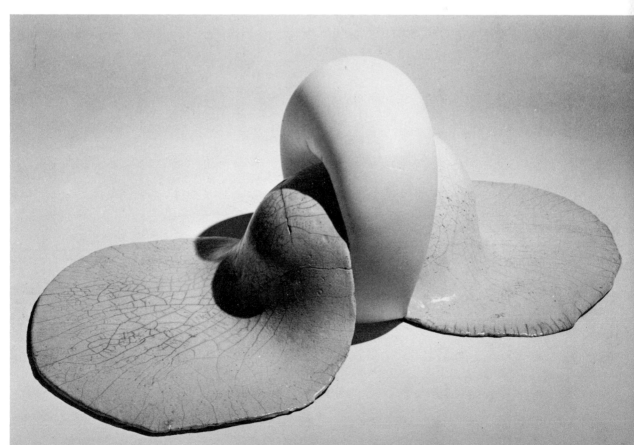

Using the Medium

Hand-built forms must be joined and constructed carefully if they are to survive the shock of a fast firing and the pressure of the tongs. The ten to fifteen percent shrinkage of clay as it dries must also be considered. When forms or supports are used, a newspaper or cloth separator should be placed between the support and the clay. This allows for easy removal and prevents the clay from sticking and eventually splitting as it dries. If a piece has not dried properly—that is evenly and slowly—it could crack or break. If the piece is too thick or if it is not thoroughly dry it might explode during the bisque firing. Special weight, size, and form limitations exist for raku ware because it must fit easily into the kiln and be easy to grasp and move with tongs; remember, it is to be removed from the kiln when still glowing hot.

I do not ask my students to create traditional Japanese tea bowls with the raku clay anymore than I could ask them to dress in a traditional Japanese kimono. What I do ask, is that they work and create from their own instinctive feelings and innermost convictions. They need not turn to the standards of beauty or the values of another place and another time

John Loree, hand built raku platter with incised design, 9" x 16".

Robert Falk, hanging raku slab planter, 12" in diameter. The clay slabs were pressed around the weathered rope which had been placed inside a bowl form.

to work in raku clay. However, I do encourage them to look at, admire, and study the pottery of other times, and the lives and philosophy of the creators of raku. It will not only serve as a source of stimulation, but it will make them more aware of the purpose of their own activities and their own lives.

An understanding and historical knowledge of the Japanese tea bowl can contribute immeasurably to the character of one's own work. To recognize the value placed on the subtle irregularity of form—the undulations

Jim Powell, wheel-thrown form, 9" x 12".

of the rim; the texture of the glaze; the shape of the shallow depression on the inside of the bowl;* and the hand-formed contour of the foot rim—will give insights into personal expression. To be in sympathy with the values placed on the tea bowl, to be sensitive to the feelings of touch, both on the lips as the tea is sipped, and in the hands as the bowl is held, is to be in unity with your own senses and inner dialogue and capable of working from your own personality. The spirit of the raku bowl is part of its shape and substance.

The realization of physical forms created from clay requires a concentrated and coordinated effort by the potter. This is especially true of raku pottery, as you will learn by experiencing the entire raku process.

* This depression was used for holding the last droplets of tea, sometimes, for measuring to determine the amount of powdered tea needed to fill that bowl.

4

Glazes and Glazing

Raku glazes are like other ceramic glazes except they are designed to mature at temperatures between 1600°F. and 2000 F°., the temperature range of most present-day raku glaze bases. Raku glazes are usually classified by their fusion temperature, but may also be classified as raw or fritted, or as highly lead or highly alkaline in composition. Raku glazes may be opaque or transparent, depending on the presence and quantity of opacifiers or colored oxides. These glazes frequently have a glassy appearance and tend to craze or form crackly patterns upon cooling. If the crazing is undesirable, it may be remedied by the addition of flint (silica). Fluid melting and excessive running are characteristic of raku glazes, but this tendency can be overcome by adding a refractory such as kaolin.

The most pleasing characteristic of the low temperature raku glaze is the wide range of color, brilliance, and intensity possible from the various coloring oxides. Copper yields rich shades of green in oxidation (firing with an excess supply of oxygen) and many metallic lusters are possible in reduction (firing with a shortage of oxygen). Iron produces soft tones of tan and if a high percentage of the oxide is used, rich ambers and reddish browns will result. When small proportions of tin oxides are added as opacifiers the result is usually a warm creamy-looking glaze. Tin oxide imparts a pleasant softness to what might otherwise be harsh colors such as those that are made with the use of cobalt oxide.

Robert Piepenburg, bisqued pots awaiting glaze.

Lead Glazes

Lead oxide is probably the most useful chemical in a raku glaze and can almost be used as a glaze, without any other substance. Colemanite (synthetic colemanite) and Gerstley Borate (natural colemanite) are equally useful but are getting hard to find since they are difficult to make or mine. Glazes fluxed with lead are useful within a wide range of firing temperature, and in fusions with the high-firing silicates they produce a glaze base that is capable of producing colors and effects that are unobtainable in any other glazes. When fired, a lead glaze has a smooth soft surface finish that may be crazed or shiny. The big disadvantage of using a raw lead glaze is that it is poisonous and may be harmful to the potter who works with it and injurious to anyone who eats or drinks from lead-glazed ware. When working with lead, simple safeguards should be followed to avoid inhaling dust or vapors. Precautions should be taken to avoid contaminating your food with dust particles and by absent-mindedly putting soiled fingers to your mouth. If you have an open cut, wear rubber or plastic gloves when mixing and applying the glaze.

History and legend indicate that lead-glazed pottery may have contributed to the decline of Roman aristocracy, and the eventual fall of the Roman Empire. Wine stored in lead-glazed vessels or drunk from lead-glazed cups could have carried lead particles. The ingesting of these lead particles may have caused sterility as a result of chronic lead poisoning. The lead-glazed Mexican pottery of today is thought to be a source of disease or disability among the segment of the Mexican poor who use it. Reports from many countries throughout the world implicate lead as a poisoning agent that can cause serious illness, especially among children.

Lead is a substance that will dissolve in a liquid. This solubility makes lead glaze particularly dangerous if used on cooking or eating utensils. The lead in all compounds is highly soluble, but it can be made almost non-toxic in a glaze by adding large amounts of silica and alumina. Flint can be used as a form of free silica. Cornwall stone (a mixture of decomposed granite, quartz, feldspar, and other earths), as well as feldspar, or aluminum oxide may be used as a form of alumina. In theory, the molecular ratio of lead to silica should be about one to two, and the ratio of alumina to silica should be between one to four and one to twelve. The alkaline

earths, particularly calcium oxide in the form of whiting, barium oxide, zinc oxide, and magnesium in the form of dolomite, will further decrease the solubility of lead.

Lead can also be made nontoxic and safe for the potter by fritting, a process of fusion with other ingredients that will create a compound of low solubility. Frit is a powdered, glassy material made by melting soluble materials, in this case lead, with other more stable or insoluble materials. The materials are heated together until they melt and fusion occurs, then they are quenched by dunking, when still liquid-hot, into water. Fragments of the brittle frit are formed. If the original ingredients were in the correct proportions, the frit is ready to be ground and safely used as a glaze.

The frit glaze should be nonpoisonous. Another advantage is it will fit the clay body better, and because the materials have already been melted and the volatiles driven off, it will melt and flow more smoothly with less bubbling and less pitting. There are many commercially made leaded frits on the market, but unfortunately, not all of them have a low solubility rate. If at all possible use leadless frits, and avoid combining them with leaded frits. Many potters will not use lead glazes or lead frits —ever.

Above, *Anne Kingsbury, raku pin cushion 19" wide. The white glaze (60% Gerstley Borate and 40% Flint), the red velvet of the pin cushion and black clay serve to accentuate and enhance each other.*

Opposite page, Mary Town (student), raku pitcher with handle, 5½" high. touch of cobalt slip was sprayed on the side of the piece before the white laze was added.

Unless a glaze contains a large proportion of lead, the lead that is in the glaze can be made insoluble by firing the glaze above cone 05 or a temperature of 1950° F. This system works well, especially if the glaze contains several of the other oxides. Although I no longer use glazes containing lead, some highly leaded glaze formulas are included in this chapter. The color characteristics they are capable of imparting are unequaled by any glazes made from nonlead formulas.

Lead glaze should not be used on pieces that might be used for eating or, even worse, drinking. Fortunately, raku pottery is not very practical for the kitchen and raku is seldom used as tableware. But if there is any concern as to the solubility or the amount of lead released by a particular glaze, the glaze can easily be tested by a number of local independent research and testing laboratories. The most accepted procedure is to treat the glazed surface with an acetic acid solution for a period of eight to twelve hours, followed by an instrumental determination or measurement with an atomic absorption spectrophotometer. The allowable maximum release of lead from a glaze is 7 ppm (seven parts per million).

Bisque Firing

Most glazing is done on bisque ware—ware that has already been fired once at about 1850° F. or to pyrometric cone 06. Bisquing removes moisture from the clay and changes it from a plastic substance that is soluble in water into a brittle substance porous enough to absorb glaze yet hard enough to be handled safely.

Many potters, respecting the traditional raku concept of softness as a quality of appearance and strength, bisque at a low temperature, such as 1640° F., or pyrometric cone 010. If the temperature is any lower than this, the ware may have to be dampened before glazing to prevent an excessive absorption of the glaze by the porous clay. Other raku potters prefer a dense clay body and have safely bisque fired at temperatures as high as 2125° F. or cone 2.

Raku is usually bisque fired in the oxidizing atmosphere of electric kilns, and care must be taken to raise the temperature very slowly, until color is visible. After color can be seen, the temperature may be safely increased about 250° F. each hour, until the desired temperature is reached. If the ware is bisque fired in a top loading electric kiln the lid should be closed and the peep holes in the kiln should be plugged before the switches are turned on and the firing is started. The fire burns away most of the organic impurities in the clay, especially in fire clays with a low mineral content and a high organic content. Leave the holes in the kiln plugged throughout the firing to reduce odors. The fumes from firing this type of clay can become noxious if the kiln or kiln room is not properly ventilated. However, if there is adequate ventilation, the peep holes should be left open for the first few hours of firing to allow moisture and chemical fumes to escape. One can leave the hinged top of the kiln partially or entirely open for the first hour or two; this procedure also prevents rapid heating and lessens the chances of the ware exploding if you are firing thick or large, heavy pieces.

Should the bisque kiln overfire and the clay vitrify and become non-absorbent, it will make glazing difficult. Syrup or commercially powdered gums can be added to the glaze. These enable the glaze to adhere to the ware; they will evaporate and burn away during the glaze firing.

Gums are sometimes added to keep the glaze from chipping or flaking off the ware, but if a potter is reasonably careful when handling his glazed pieces, the use of gum can be avoided. Gum might also be added to a glaze that is going to be used over an already glazed and fired area. However, gum is usually unnecessary if the reglazing is done with a glaze containing a high percentage of clay, or if it is done right after the firing, when the pot is hot enough to hold the new glaze by causing the immediate evaporation of the water that is in the glazing solution. Raku pots can be reglazed and refired several times, but with each succeeding firing the chance for breakage multiplies. Reglazed pieces have a better chance for survival if they are refired immediately while still warm from the previous firing. If they have cooled, it then becomes safer to refire them at a later time when they can be included in the first firing of a cold kiln.

Some raku potters eliminate the separate bisque fire and fire glazed greenware to maturity in their electric or gas kilns. They slowly bring the temperature up to about 1700° F. over a five or six hour period. This one-fire method is the exception, however, and I only mention it because it calls for adjustments and adaptations in the glaze formulas. These adaptations are necessary because clay—especially greenware—and glaze expand and contract at different rates when heated. Most raku glaze formulas that are adapted for a single firing contain ten to twenty percent bentonite, or twenty-five to thirty-five percent ball clay.

Preparing the Glaze

Glazing raku is like glazing earthenware or stoneware pottery. Pieces can be glazed using the standard techniques—pouring, dipping, brushing, and spraying. Pouring, dipping, and brushing are the easiest methods to master, and require the least equipment. Spraying has many advantages but if the glaze contains lead, it has the disadvantage of creating a lead vapor or toxic atmosphere in a spray booth that is not adequately ventilated. A powerful exhaust fan must be used when spray glazing with a lead base glaze.

Raku glazes, like raku clay bodies, can be bought commercially prepared. However, if you want to save money and get closer to your craft, you might avoid them. There are times when exceptions might be made: a few four-ounce jars of a brushing glaze that is applied in three coats, cone range 04 to 07, might be purchased to add a luscious tangerine, silver, or sanguine accent to a piece. It is often almost impossible to obtain such specific colors with your own glaze mixture, unless you resort to adding commercial glaze stains.

It is not particularly exciting nor fun to mix and make a batch of glazes, but it is easy and it involves the potter with ceramic chemicals and chemical formula calculations. The procedure simply requires the weighing out of each raw material—in grams, mixing the ingredients with water, and finally screening the entire solution through a 50 mesh sieve. Some of the coarser materials, such as granular borax or sodium uranate, may have to be added after sieving.

A quick and easy way to make up a batch of raku glaze is to recalculate the formulas so that the raw materials are added to the water by volume and not by weight—in a manner similar to using a cooking recipe.

The consistency of a glaze has a direct influence on color and surface texture. The glaze must be exactly right, resembling somewhat the pouring consistency of cream—thick enough to just reveal the outline of your fingernail when your finger is covered with glaze. Glazes should be stirred, mixed, or shaken before each use. The chemicals have a tendency to settle to the bottom in a matter of minutes leaving the water at the top of the container. Glazes that have not been used, but left sitting around the studio for a year or longer, should be tested by firing on small clay tiles and checked. The glaze materials may decompose and cause defects in the final glazed surface and color. I once reprocessed about 4,000 grams of a raku glaze that had stood unmixed for nine months. Additional water was

Student brushing commercial glazes on a plaque that will be raku fired.

Glaze being mixed with a wire whip before it is used. Note the plastic gloves worn to protect the hands from the lead glaze.

added, and then the glaze was stirred and resieved. The glaze was restored to the consistency of the original formula but the results were totally different from the glaze that was first used. Fortunately, it did work—in some ways it was more interesting than the original glaze—and did not have to be thrown out.

Applying the Glaze

The effects that can be obtained with glazes are limitless—each glaze can be changed with the use of slips, engobes, underglazes, stains, powdered oxide rubs, ochre washes, resists, and brush decorations.

The way the glaze is applied should be determined by the shape of the pot and the creative insights of the potter. The methods of glazing should not be thought of separately from the ceramic form to be glazed. Application and form should be indistinguishable. They work together as an entity—each holding fulfillment for the other. A form should not be dipped to cover it with a glaze, but should be dipped to compliment its contour and feeling. This may mean a quick splash into the glaze, or a gentle lowering at an angle. It may mean immersing the pot several times in the same glaze, or into glazes of different colors overlapping areas and exciting and subtle variations of color and shading.

The same is true in glazes that are applied by pouring—use a color and a technique that is compatible to the form being glazed. When pouring the glaze, it should be spontaneously cascaded on the clay form and allowed to freely follow and capitalize on its contour. If more than one coat of glaze is to be used, each coat should be applied when the preceding coat is still slightly damp. If the base coat of glaze is allowed to dry completely, parts of the glaze may crack and flake off, or still worse crawl in the firing.

Glazes that have been applied more thickly than one-sixteenth of an inch may run down the sides of the piece and form a pool inside. When this happens be sure that the piece is level while cooling. Thickly applied glaze may also drip down the outside of the piece to the foot and puddle on the kiln shelf. To keep the shelf and bottom of a pot free of runny glaze do not glaze three-quarters of an inch on the bottom of the pot. Wax or paraffin may be applied to the foot of a pot to prevent the foot from absorbing glaze. The wax will ignite and burn away as soon as the pot is placed into the hot kiln. Probably being very careful and neat when you apply the glaze and removing any excess with a clean, damp sponge is the best way to avoid glazed incrusted kiln shelves and pot bottoms.

Lusters

Some potters use metallic or lustery effects as part of their glazing. Lusters are light coatings of metal or metal oxides on the surface of the glaze. Iridescent sheens can be achieved in reduction immediately following the glaze firing, and come from metal oxides such as copper sulfate, copper carbonate, silver carbonate, bismuth sub-nitrate, and silver nitrate. Metal oxides may be applied to an already glazed but unfired surface by brushing

*Pouring glaze inside a form
with the aid of a funnel.*

*Glazing the inside:
the glaze is poured out
with a quick rotating motion.*

Glazing the outside of the pot
by pouring. The glaze
bucket can be used as
the container to catch the overflow.

The best time to reglaze a raku pot
is right after it has been fired
or reduced when it is still
hot enough to dry the
new glaze completely
in just a few minutes.

Charles Green (student), raku sun and rainclouds. The 8" diameter sun is decorated with commercial orange glazes; the clouds are white with blue leather fringe.

or spraying before the glaze firing. Both lead and alkaline glazes can be used under lusters, although some darkening of color may occur if the glaze contains a great deal of lead or dark colorants. Metal oxides can also be added to the base glaze in small percentages. For example, two percent of silver nitrate can be added to a white glaze to obtain a gold luster. A different percentage of bismuth, sub-nitrate, or uranium oxide might also be added to the same glaze for a heightened reflective surface. For painted effects try a solution of 10 grams of silver nitrate to 50 cubic centimeters of water. However, this mixture must be used within a day or two after preparation—it weakens rather quickly. Many raku luster glazed surfaces have a tendency to fade if not vanish altogether months after the firing.

As you become more experienced and a more meaningful and intimate relationship with raku is established, you may well come to feel as I do that the black reduced clay body is beautiful in itself and in need of little or no glaze. However raku is an individual matter. It has a strong tradition but holds no rigid rules or standard of values for individual self-expression, other than that feelings should be natural and honest. It would be very appropriate for the raku potter to develop his own philosophy and approach toward glazing and not glazing.

Glaze Formulas

Several raku glaze formulas are given on the following pages. The base materials are listed first, and then the colorants are given. The glaze materials should be added to water by weight and then sieved. Glazes from these formulas have been used successfully as they are and in combination with other formulas. Each glaze matures at a slightly different temperature, and the results may not be exactly the same for every firing. This is due to human and mechanical variables, such as method of application, thickness of glaze, type of kiln, kiln temperature, reduction techniques used, and even weather. It is advisable to keep a glazing notebook and to include a quick but descriptive sketch of each piece with a list entry of the glaze or glazes used and the way in which they were applied, as well as the other variable factors.

RAKU SURFACE PATINAS: COR-TEN SERIES

(Note—These measurements are by volume and the recipes may be left in a pre-mixed powdered state to be sprinkled or thrown on the surface of bisque ware that has been sprayed with water. The result should be a crusty metallic anti-glaze surface that is compatible with black body reduction and certain clay forms.)

Weiser Rust

5½ Colemanite
1¼ Nepheline Synenite
1⅞ Copper Carbonate
½ Black Nickel Oxide
½ Tin Oxide

Copper Sand

8 Gerstley Borate
2 Bone Ash
½ Copper Carbonate
¼ Cobalt Oxide
⅛ Tin Oxide

Blue Velvet Crust

3 Gerstley Borate
1 Nepheline Synenite
2 Aluminum Oxide
2 Cobalt Oxide
2 Dark Tone Rutile

Dry Mo-Town Rust

3 Gerstley Borate
1 Nepheline Synenite
2 Cornwall Stone
2 Nickel Oxide
2 Copper Carbonate

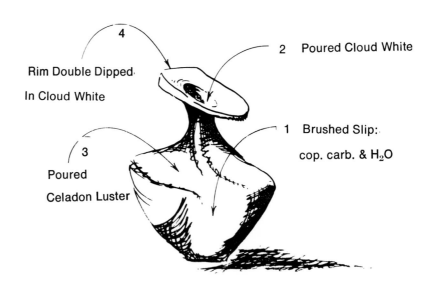

4 Rim Double Dipped In Cloud White

2 Poured Cloud White

3 Poured Celadon Luster

1 Brushed Slip: cop. carb. & H_2O

Sample sketch, as might be found in a glazing notebook, showing glazes used.

RAKU GLAZE FORMULAS

(Note—All measurements are in percentages)

Piepenburg Cloud White
75 Colemanite
25 Feldspar

Piepenburg #3
40 Ferro Frit 3134
40 Red Lead
20 Flint

A—Celadon Luster
5 Manganese Dioxide
3 Copper Carbonate

B—Puce Copper
4 Black Copper Oxide

C—Metallic Red Luster
3 Black Uranium Oxide
2 Black Copper Oxide

D—Pale Aqua Luster
3 Copper Carbonate
1/10 Cobalt Oxide

E—Purple Amber
1½ Manganese Dioxide
1/10 Cobalt Oxide

Piepenburg Streaked Burgundy
25 Ferro Frit 3134
25 Colemanite
25 Nepheline Syenite
25 Red Lead
4 Tin Oxide
4 Manganese Dioxide

Smi-Matt Black
45 Ferro Frit 3134
40 White Lead
15 Flint
4 Red Iron Oxide
3 Manganese Dioxide
2 Cobalt Oxide

Cathy's Rabbit Fur
50 Borax
40 Ferro Frit 3134
10 Kaolin
5 Antimony Oxide
3 Nickel Oxide

Raye's Dalmation Matt
60 Colemanite
18 Pyrophylite
11 Opax
11 Granular Illumenite

Loree #2
60 Colemanite
30 Red Lead
5 Nepheline Syenite
5 Kaolin
> **A—Brandy**
> 7½-8 Red Iron Oxide
> **B—Cerebral Luster**
> 2½ Black Copper Oxide

Piepenburg 50-50
50 Ferro Frit 3134
50 Colemanite
> **A—Oil Luster**
> 2½ Black Copper Oxide
> 1 Manganese Dioxide
> **B—Red Bronze**
> 3 Tin Oxide
> 2½ Black Copper Oxide

Maroon Rootbeer
50 Ferro Frit 3134
50 White Lead
22 Ochre
2 Red Iron Oxide

RAKU #5
90 Red Lead
10 Flint

A—Yellow Green to Red Luster
3 Copper Carbonate
1 Red Iron Oxide

B—Green to Maroon Luster
3 Copper Carbonate

C—Yellow to Black
8 Sodium Uranate

D—Speckled Yellow Black
5 Black Uranium Oxide

E—Speckled Brown
4 Potassium Bichromate
6 Sodium Uranate

F—Burnt Golden Umber
5 Antimony Oxide
2 Green Nickel Oxide

G—Yellow Brown
4 Tin Oxide
4 Manganese Dioxide

H—Olivacious Green
½ Cobalt Carbonate
3 Black Uranium Oxide
2 Spanish Red Iron

I—Forest Green
3 Red Lead Chromate

J—Off Blue
7 Tin Oxide
⅓ Cobalt Oxide

K—Muddy Copper
5 Manganese Dioxide
3 Copper Carbonate

L—Soft Black
3 Manganese Dioxide
4 Red Iron Oxide
1 Cobalt Oxide

M—Dark Reddish Orange
8 Potassium Bichromate

N—Pale Yellow

8 Tin Oxide

½ Manganese Dioxide

O—Soft Dark Brown

20 Umber

P—Brown Orange

5 Potassium Bichromate

Piepenburg Soft

45 Ferro Frit 3134

45 White Lead

10 Flint

A—Soft Blue

7 Tin Oxide

⅓ Cobalt Oxide

B—Soft Yellow Copper

2 Tin Oxide

2 Black Copper Oxide

C—Soft Blue Copper

2 Black Copper Oxide

½ Cobalt Carbonate

D—Soft Black

30 Yellow Ochre

Y-4 Lemon Yellow

55 White Lead

25 Ferro Frit 3134

20 Flint

2 Red Lead Chromate

Middlebrook's Barium Crackle White

60 Gerstley Borate

50 Potash Feldspar

22 Barium Carbonate

16 Silica

Hank's Raconeat

55 Colemanite

20 Nepheline Syenite

15 Lithium Carbonate

5 Kaolin (E.P.K.)

5 Tin Oxide

Smoky Metal

40 Colemanite

30 Ferro Frit 3134

20 Flint

5 Ball Clay

5 Whiting

Mecham White

80 Colemanite

20 Cornwall Stone

A—Deep Purple

4 Manganese Dioxide

1 Cobalt Oxide

B—Carey's Copper Penny

8 Ochre

2 Black Copper Oxide

1 Cobalt Oxide

C—DelFavero Luster

2 Copper Carbonate

D—2-1 Luster

½ Black Copper Oxide

¼ Cobalt Carbonate

E—Dragon Gray

1 Red Iron Oxide

¼ Cobalt Carbonate

F—Copper Cobalt Luster

¼ Cobalt Carbonate

2 Copper Carbonate

G—Orchard Ridge Luster

½ Black Copper Oxide

4 Light Tone Rutile

H—Gold Luster

2 Silver Nitrate

1 Tin Oxide

Hendry Base

50 Gerstley Borate

50 Borax

Soldner Base

80 Gerstley Borate

20 Nepheline Syenite

Piepenburg 4-6 Base

60 Gerstley Borate
40 Potash Feldspar

A—Payne's Gray

¼ Cobalt Carbonate
3 Spanish Red Iron

R.P.—3 Raku Base

75 Gerstley Borate
20 Flint
5 Kaolin

A—Winter Gray

6 Umber
8 Tin Oxide

J.P. Metallic

65 Colemanite
25 Anhydrous Borax
5 Nepheline Syenite
5 Kaolin
5 Light Tone Rutile
2 Black Copper Oxide

Neumann Engobe (by volume)

1 part Kaolin (E.P.K.)
1 part Silica
½ part Nepheline Syenite
¼ part Ball Clay

Soldner Stain

50 Copper
50 Iron

Listed at the end of this chapter, on page 100, are several raku base glaze formulas that can be used for color experiments. These formulas are separated into two categories, lead and nonlead bases. They may be transparent, opaque, crackly, glossy, shiny, or semi-matt shades of off-white, and they are excellent vehicles for color. I hope, however, that you will develop some base formulas from your own experiments. If you are not sure what each chemical will do, or how it will contribute to a glaze, you can easily find out by firing each chemical on a separate test tile and keep these tiles to use for future reference. The strong fluxing power of colemanite, the high refractory qualities of kaolin, or other properties of still other chemicals can be studied and the results used to suggest proportions or combinations of chemicals that might lead to a new base glaze formula of your own.

One relatively simple way to begin your experiments with color in a base glaze is to use the 50-50 color bland method; this requires fifteen test tiles made from your raku clay body. To make these tiles, roll a slab of clay that is a quarter of an inch thick, cut fifteen strips, 1½" x 4" each, from this slab. The strips should be bent in the form of an L so they can stand upright in the kiln and then left to dry. Freestanding pinch tiles or tiles that are cut from a wheel-thrown tile ring are other types of tiles that might be easier for you to fashion and use.

A good way to keep a set of glazed tiles together for future reference is to string them on a short length of cord. If you want to do this, a hole, one-quarter of an inch in diameter, should be made through the top of each tile while it is leather hard and before it is glazed and fired.

The following is a glazing procedure used for experimenting with color in base glaze formulas:

Color Test Chart

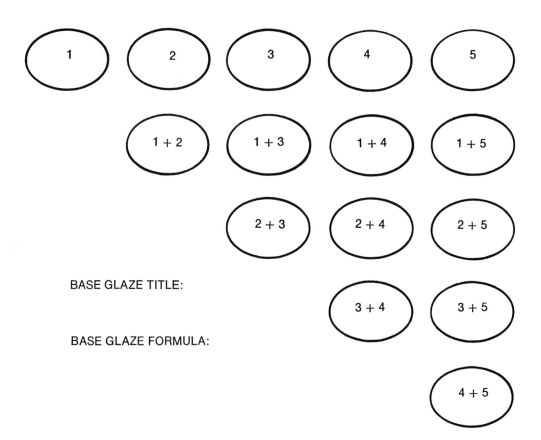

BASE GLAZE TITLE:

BASE GLAZE FORMULA:

Procedure

1. Choose the base glaze.
2. Choose the color oxides that you want to use, and determine the amount of each oxide you want to use.
3. Make a chart, similar to the one above, and write in the colorants and percentages of each to be used.
4. Identify and record the information that will be needed. Note it on the back of each tile while the tiles are still wet, or leather hard. The information should include the base glaze that will be used and the amount—in percent—of the color oxides that will be used.

5. Dry and bisque fire the tiles.

6. Mix 150 grams of the base glaze.

7. Label fifteen paper cups to correspond with the chart on page 94 and the colorants that you want to test. Put 10 grams of base glaze into each of the fifteen paper cups.

8. Add to the 10 grams of base glaze in each cup the appropriate percentage of colorant. Remember: 1 percent of 10 grams is not one gram, but 1/10th (one-tenth) of a gram. Mathematically, 1% is always expressed decimally as .01 and anything less than 1% has two decimal places to the left of it. Example: ¼% is written decimally as .0025.

9. Carefully add water to the glaze in each cup, until a creamy consistency is obtained, and stir.

10. By pouring directly from each paper cup, or by brushing, apply the glaze to the upper two-thirds of the front of each tile. Two applications of glaze should be used to insure dense and even coverage on the top third of the tile.

The glaze tiles must be treated and fired in the same manner as other glazed ware. They should be completely dry before the glaze firing, and a few of the test tiles should be placed in each kiln load with regular firings. If all of the tiles are in the same kiln, the last few tiles to be taken out of the kiln would have oxidized for too long a time for them to validly respond to a post firing reduction.

If you want to test for oxidation and reduction on the same tile, sink half of it into an open pile of dry sawdust as soon as it is removed from the kiln. The unburied portion of the tile should give some indication of how the glaze will look when it is allowed to oxidize, the buried half will show the effects of reduction, and the possibilities for lusters. When the tiles have cooled, they should be examined and the results of the experiment should be recorded with any additional notes concerning differences in color or texture that resulted from the post-firing treatment. The charts on pages 98 and 99 might be used to record this information.

In making your evaluation of the glazes, be alert to any possible color combinations that might prove successful. Would a different proportion of oxides or a different combination of chemicals mean a more exciting glaze? Follow your intuition and your own insights; if they are pursued they will often lead to the serendipitous development of beautiful glazes, which often defy logical analysis. Experiment, and use your imagination—but don't forget to keep careful records so that you will be able to produce similar results again, if you want to.

Pouring an experimental raku glaze on a test tile for future reference.

*Ruth Ellen, Pink Raku Pot-Bottle,
slab and wheel-thrown with a matt
salmon-pink gerstley borate glaze, 10" high.*

*Steven and Susan Kemenyffy, Mustard Maya, 24" wide. Bisqued at cone
01 and glaze fired over a two to three hour period.*

GLAZE TITLE		Frit	White Lead	Flint	Colemanite	Nepheline Syenite	Red Lead	Feldspar	Cornwall Stone	Kaolin	Gerstley Borate	Borax		
	1													
	2													
	3													
	4													
	6													
	7													
	8													
	9													
	11													
	12													
	13													
	14													
	16													
	17													
	18													
	19													
	21													
	22													
	23													
	24													
	26													
	27													
	28													
	29													
	30													

Potassium Bichromate	Tin Oxide	Uranium	Cobalt Carbonate	Manganese Dioxide	Cobalt Oxide	Rutile	Nickel Oxide	Copper Oxide	Red Iron Oxide	Chrome Oxide	Sodium Uranate	Copper Carbonate	GLAZE DESCRIPTION

Chart for recording glaze test data and personal recipes

NON-LEADED RAKU BASE GLAZES

Title	Frit	Flint	Colemanite	Nepheline Syenite	Feldspar	Gerstley Borate	Kaolin	Cornwall Stone	Borax	Ball Clay
G—14			60	20	20					
L—1			70	10	10		10			
R—5	35	10	40				15			
R—6	40	10	40				10			
B—11					25	75				
E—8			25			75				
W—2						20		40	70	
F—1						85			10	5
G.B.						100				
P—4					40	60				

LEADED RAKU BASE GLAZES

Title	Frit	Flint	Red Lead	Colemanite	Kaolin	Nepheline Syenite	Borax	White Lead		
B—2	40	10						50		
B—5	45	15						40		
Z—13	80							20		
H—12		20	70		10					
K—5	15		15	55		15				
U—1	10	20						70		
V—7	25	20						55		
M—13		30			3		15	52		
I—13	30	16	54							
X—5	35	30						35		

5

Kilns

Raku kilns, like other kilns, are structures designed to accumulate heat. The heat may originate from a resistance and be radiated as it is in electric kilns, or it may come from the combustion of a fuel mixed with air or oxygen as in wood burning or gas kilns.

Kilns are usually constructed of materials that are resistant to heat and that will act as insulators, keeping the heat within the kiln.

Kiln Materials

The structures themselves can be built from any number of fire-resistant refractory materials, and can be constructed in a variety of shapes. Bricks are made from compounds of refractories, and are the most common structural material used, so most kilns are built in a variation of the box shape. Kilns are often designed to use standard-size bricks with a minimum of cutting. The standard brick shape is the nine inch straight which is a brick 2½" x 4½" x 9".

Most designers and builders of raku kilns choose either soft insulating

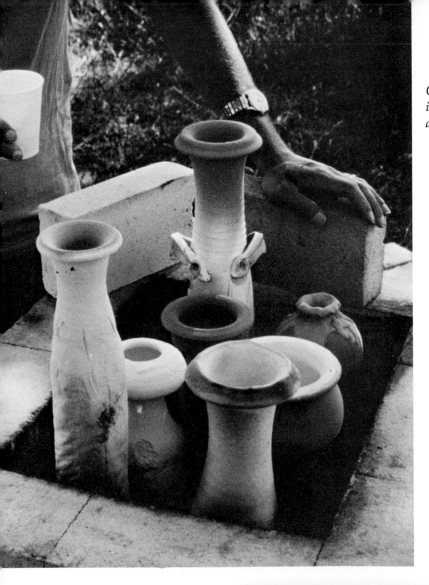

Glazed raku ware tightly loaded
in the kiln before the sides
are built up and the burner lit.

Maria Carter, three raku forms.
They were made of a stoneware
body, and were fired by bringing
the temperature in an electric kiln
up gradually over a period of
several hours—until the correct
maturing temperature is reached.

Paul Soldner (the gentleman wearing the bowler) lowering his oil-fired fulcrumed kiln.

Raku kiln with a counter-balanced door and roll-out floor built by David Middlebrook. The walls and floor are cast with a composition of crushed soft brick and lumnite cement; the arch is brick. The interior height from the floor to the arch is 56".

firebrick or hard firebrick. They are refractory brick and are suitable at temperatures beyond those used for raku. Common building brick, or red brick, can be used if it is laid in double-thick rows. However, these bricks have the drawback of excessive cracking, and heat loss.

Soft or insulating firebricks are excellent for kiln materials and are far more effective than other bricks, due to a myriad of entrapped air bubbles. Raku kilns made of soft firebricks do not take nearly as long to heat to the proper temperatures as do kilns made from other materials. This makes little difference in the quality of the glazes being fired, but it is a matter of fuel economics. It is difficult to say just how much heat loss is involved—with 4½-inch-thick hard bricks temperatures as high as 600° F. can occur on the outside wall of raku kilns, whereas soft brick kilns of the same wall thickness will register temperatures only half as high.

Insulating bricks are graded according to the temperature they will be able to withstand without deforming. Some brick manufacturers and suppliers have their own symbols or letter codes to designate the firing temperatures for their bricks. For example, a G-20 brick is usable at temperatures up to 2000° F., a G-23 brick, up to 2300° F., and so forth.

Frank Colson's liftable drum raku kiln. This light-weight kiln consists of a bottomless steel drum lined with a one-half inch thick Fiberfrax Lo-Con Blanket, one of the many refractory fibrous materials put out by the Carborundum Company. The material, which is recommended for use up to 2300° F. (but will not melt until 3200° F.) is glued to the inside of the drum with a Fiberfrax coating cement.

One advantage of a top loading kiln is that it can easily be built up to accommo- date all forms by us- ing additional bricks.

Right, *Kurt Weiser, 28" high raku form that was wrapped in salt-soaked burlap, held in place by copper wire, and fired. This pot was stacked among several other pots in a wood-burning kiln.*

If you decide to use hard firebricks you can expect them to be thirty or forty percent less expensive than the soft firebrick, and the hard brick should last much longer than the soft, especially if the kiln is outdoors and exposed to weather. Hard firebrick is very dense, heavy, and durable; it is much more resistant to crumbling and weather than the more porous and lighter soft insulating brick.

The Fuel

Some potters prefer to fire electric kilns even though the raku technique is hard on the kiln elements. Wood burning kilns are appreciated and valued by many and have a traditional Japanese heritage. Wood burning, like charcoal burning, kilns require a great deal of time and effort to fire, and, once they get started, produce great quantities of smoke.

Fuel oil is inexpensive, but it is dirty and smelly. Fuel oil is a liquid which must be converted into a vapor before combustion can take place, and this means that it is difficult to start a fire and to keep the fire burning until the kiln has reached a red heat. If fuel oil is used to fire a raku kiln, forced air from a paddle-wheel blower or vacuum cleaner will be needed for an efficient gas-air mixture.

Natural gas works well as a fuel and should be used if the kiln is located near a gas meter. If you are not near a meter it can be expensive to have the utility company install a line and an additional meter. However, once the pipe and the meter are installed, it is much cheaper and safer to use natural gas than to use propane gas. If you fire with natural gas you never have to worry about losing pressure or running out of fuel during a firing. Natural gas kilns fire well when the gas is blended with forced air obtained from such sources as old or used vacuum cleaners or portable hair dryers. The air and gas lines can simply be laid adjacent to one another at the mouth of the burner port or, better yet, the gas line can be bent, positioned, and centered in the path of the air flow. Propane gas is a liquified petroleum gas that is delivered, stored in, and used from tanks that always seem to need refilling. Another problem during the operation of the tanks is that gas is continually being created by the vaporization of the liquid. If too much liquid evaporates into gas at one time, the remaining liquid in the tank freezes because of the temperature drop that accompanies evaporation; when this happens, pressure is lost.

Natural Gas

Forced Air

Gas Valve

Metal Strap

Copper Tubing

Black Iron Pipe

Flexible Air Hose

Forced-Air Natural Gas Burner

To insure enough pressure, especially if you fire very often, 100-pound tanks should be used preferably in tandem. Each 100-pound tank should provide eight to ten hours of firing. If you have trouble during a firing, enough pressure to finish the firing can usually be obtained by turning a freezing tank on its side. This trick is very useful if there are no back-up or reserved tanks. Although there are many problems with vaporizing propane gas, I prefer it as a source of heat for firing my raku kilns.

Propane, unlike natural gas, is heavier than air. If a leak should occur around a hose fitting or at a tank valve, as has happened to me on two occasions with newly delivered tanks, the gas will collect and cling near the ground. Because of this, the tanks should not be located indoors or within twenty or thirty feet of basements or other sunken enclosures. If the tanks are to be stored in a specially designed outbuilding or shed, air vents should be installed at floor level. Local codes and safety regulations do exist, and your supplier should know what they are and be able to advise you on the building and ventilating of any enclosure you choose.

The Burner

You can buy burners, regulators, gauges, spark lighters, high pressure hoses, and fittings from most propane suppliers. The propane burners I designed for my own use were made from black iron pipe fittings that can be found in most hardware stores for one-fourth the cost of commercially made burners. The flange burner makes use of two one and one-half inch flanges, which are separated by flat washers, and provide the air needed for the proper combustion of the gas. The half-inch gas pipe enters the flange and is held in place by a reducing bushing with three equally spaced

Hal Riegger, Viet Nam, raku face, 8″ diameter; this piece was fired in a wood-burning kiln.

Up-draft raku kiln built into the ground by Frank Kulasiewicz. Natural gas is used with a forced air blower to fire-off the ware in three to seven minutes. Cactus are often used here as a combustible for post firing reductions.

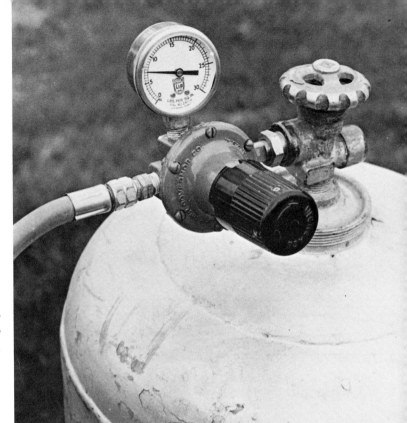

If attached to the propane tank, a high pressure regulator and 30-pound gauge will allow the potter more control in the firing of his kiln.

Getting ready to light the flange burner with a spark lighter.

5/16" x 1¼" Machine Bolt (2)

5/16" Flat Washer (6)

½" Orifice Cap—#53 Drill (.0595)

Needle Valve

½" x ¼" Reducing Coupling

1½" x 8" Nipple

1½" Flange (2)

¼" x 20 Set Screw (3)

½" x 12" Nipple

1½" x ¾" Reducing Bushing—Drill & Tap for 3, ¼" × 20 Set Screws

Propane Flange Burner

Drill or Cut 4 Air Holes

2" x 1½" Reducing Coupling

½" x ¼" Reducing Coupling

2" x 6" Nipple

1½" x ½" Reducing Bushing

½" x 8" Nipple

½" x 2" Nipple

½" Orifice Cap—1/16" Drill (.0625)

Needle Valve:

(¼" Pipe Thd. to a Left-hand Reverse Flare)

Propane Coupling Burner

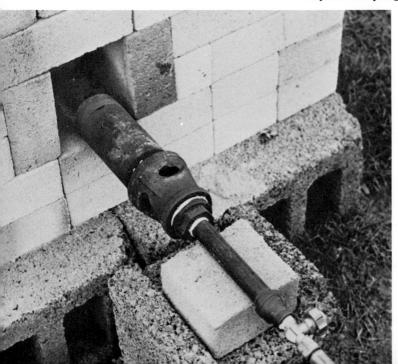

Coupling burner positioned just inside burner po...

set screws. The gas pipe is fitted—at the closed end—with an orifice made from a drilled pipe cap.

By varying the number of spacer-washers between the flanges, the air intake can be adjusted. If several washers are used a strong oxidizing atmosphere is created and the burner will draw in more than enough air, which means a hard and hot flame, and more heat. The same effect can be achieved by using an orifice made with a smaller drill. If a large orifice were used, a strong reduction atmosphere would exist because there would be a higher proportion of gas to air than needed for effective combustions. The flame would then be soft and cool. The position of the gas pipe is made adjustable by the use of thumb or set screws so that the orifice can always be set and secured just ahead of the air inlet should it be readjusted. This type of flexibility is helpful with homemade burners since some experimenting, adjusting, and even readjusting, usually has to be done. An additional advantage is that the orifice size can be quickly, easily, and inexpensively changed by simply replacing the drilled pipe cap. By increasing the diameter of the orifice hole in the pipe cap this burner can be efficiently used with natural gas.

The coupling burner is less flexible; the size of the air holes and the positioning of the orifice cannot be easily changed. The burner must be fully assembled and the position of the orifice determined before the air holes can be marked and cut with an oxyacetylene cutting torch. To insure against gas leaks, all pipe joints, up to and including the orifice cap, must be coated with pipe dope or Teflon pipe tape and securely fastened. The brass needle valve connecting the burner to the hose is optional, but if it is used, the joint between the brass and iron fittings must be covered with dope. The brass to brass, or valve to hose-fitting joint, is of the same material and self-sealing and needs only tightening.

A Good Location

Before construction of a kiln can begin, a suitable location must be found. The kiln site is important in that it can, like weather, play a big role in setting the mood for the entire firing experience. It is, by far, a more rewarding and enriching experience to raku fire your ware in a kiln situated on a sandy plateau in the fields, in a wooded glen, or near a stream, than to fire in a garage or a cluttered alley. (Although I must admit that I have had some good pots and treasure some happy memories from firings done in, of all places, a Detroit junkyard.) The experience of firing frequently transcends the act of waiting for a kiln to reach maturing temperature for unloading. The firing often approaches an interrelatedness not only with one's pottery and every other part of the creative process, but with all things, from the murmur of the summer wind near the kiln, to the murmur of the sense of life within ourselves.

If the kiln is in a location where there are a minimum of unwanted and unnatural distractions to resist, the entire experience should be very pleasant. Attention can openly be given to the moment, whether it be one of silence, of conversation or a thought on life. Many memorable moments can be had with friends and refreshments during a firing session, whether it be early morning, late afternoon, or in the evening by gas lantern if the setting and atmosphere are right.

The inner experiences of raku are best enjoyed in the exterior settings of nature. The location of the raku kiln site should be more than just a practical matter.

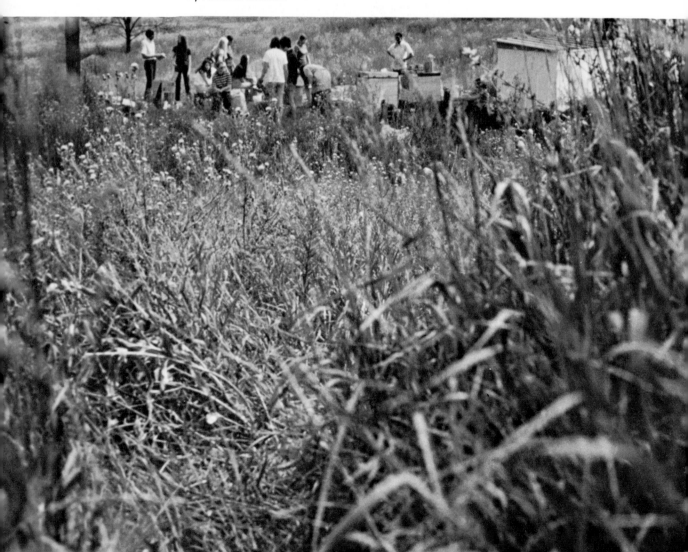

Robert Piepenburg, thrown-form with a coleorhiza-like slab top and "Gnurdols", 16" high. The impressions in the lower glazed area are the results of a post firing reduction in dry straw.

Robert Piepenburg, altered wheel- and rib-thrown form with a slab top, 9" high. The irregular glaze effect was consciously achieved by spattering the top of the piece with a large glaze-soaked sponge.

Raku counter-balanced beam kiln. The domed top was cast over a skylight form and eight cast refractory panels were used to make the octagonal wall. Pyrex sheets were used in the six window ports; however, they blistered and became smoke filled.

Jim Schultz, raku slab construction, 18" high.

Building the Kiln

The ground itself can serve as the foundation for a raku kiln. However, it may be wiser to support the kiln on a raised foundation made from hollow concrete blocks. If the kiln is built outdoors, a foundation will keep the mud and rain away from the lower part of the kiln. If the kiln is built indoors, on a concrete slab, hollow concrete blocks provide an air space that prevents the heat of the kiln fire from dehydrating, cracking, or, in extreme cases, causing the concrete slab to explode. If bare ground

Building the walls of a raku kiln with stringer courses of soft brick. Note the absence of mortar between the overlapping joints. Soft insulating bricks are accurately cut into a uniform size and can be used without mortar, whereas hard fire bricks are cast shapes and vary in the size and squareness. Frequently they require a water-fire-clay-sand mortar mixture to fill the joints and level the courses.

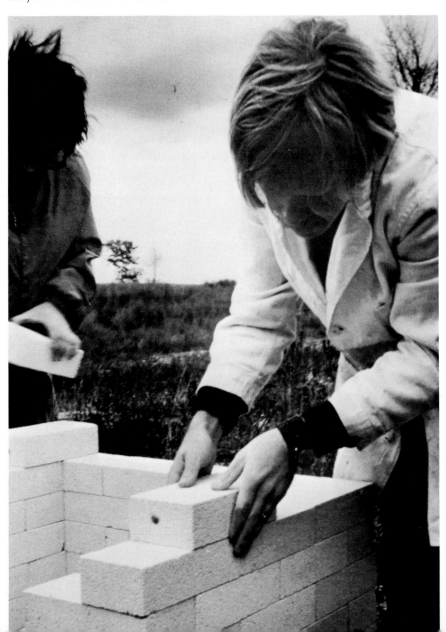

is used as a foundation for the kiln walls, it can also serve as the floor for the kiln, but if concrete blocks are used one or two layers of bricks are needed for the kiln floor. These flooring bricks prevent the concrete blocks from severe cracking and also act as insulators keeping the heat inside the kiln where it is needed.

Soft bricks for the kiln wall are laid without mortar and are held in place by their own weight. An interlocking and stronger wall is obtained if the joints are alternated or staggered so that the bricks do not align. At times it may be necessary to use half bricks to achieve this overlapping at joints and corners.

Soft brick can be cut in half with a carpenter's ripsaw in a matter of seconds using another brick as a guide to get them cut in half evenly. Hard brick has to be scored, especially at the corners. Once it is scored it can be broken using a mason's chisel and a sharp hammer blow. As the walls are being erected, at least two good-sized observation holes should be built in the sides of the kiln. These holes should be at different heights from the ground. The progress and length of the firing is determined entirely by eye—a view of the kiln's interior is necessary for a good firing.

When it comes to determining the design for a kiln you should plan for quick and easy removal of the ware. If pieces are not removed immediately after the kiln is opened they will oxidize, and reduction in the post firing will not succeed. Car kilns and liftable drum-like kilns are good because the ware is accessible from all sides and from above the kiln. Small kilns with room for one or two small pieces work best, but if the kiln is large enough to fire several pieces at once, it should have the widest door or opening that is possible.

If a standard size commercial kiln shelf is used, the design of the kiln should provide for one or two inch minimum clearance on all sides of the kiln between the shelf and the walls. A one-half- or three-quarter-inch thick, high-temperature silicone carbide shelf works well, but it is expensive. Hard fire brick works equally as well and has the added advantage of being economical to replace. Shelves are normally supported at a height of four and one-half inches above the floor of the kiln. Half bricks are used to support the shelves at this height, and if a commercial shelf does crack, or break, it can still be used by placing a supporting half brick under the broken joint.

The standard kiln wash of water added to equal parts of flint and kaolin clay work very well in protecting the shelf from drops of glaze that may stick to the shelf. The only disadvantage is that the shelf will need to be scraped and recoated after most glaze firings. An alternate but dubious

Soft insulating bricks can be cut in half with four to five strokes of a rip saw. Another brick is used as a guide.

The homemade "Alfred" type burner made with two inch pipe is mounted directly on the barrel and moves up and down with the kiln.

Commercial weed burner used by Penny Fleming for firing her Fiberfrax Lo-Con felt lined drum kiln. This three-gallon unit uses kerosene or #2 diesel fuel and has a three hour burning capacity. Note: For a lighter more portable kiln expanded metal can be used in place of the steel drum as a supporting form and the Lo-Con felt attached with two-inch homemade kanthal wire staples or ties.

Unloading a corbel walled car kiln. A single brick deflects the flame and prevents it from hitting the ware which rests directly on the car floor.

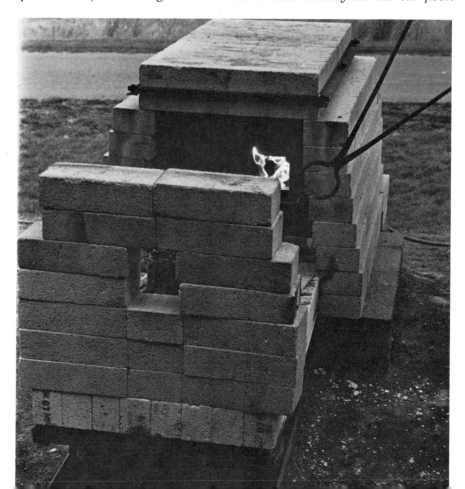

solution is to cover the shelf with two sheets of asbestos that have been cut to the same size as the shelf. The asbestos sheets will protect the shelf in the same way as a tablecloth protects the top of a table. Two layers are used because asbestos boards crack easily and a crack would expose the kiln shelf to runny glazes, the second sheet is used to overlap any breaks and add some extra protection.

Burner ports are usually four and one-half or five inches square and are built to be level with the kiln floor. When possible they should be made to face into the prevailing wind, which will act as a blower and, on very windy days, help to save fuel. The burner itself does not actually go into the opening but remains just outside where it can be cooled by the incoming secondary air. If the burner was inserted into the kiln opening, the part that was inside the kiln would eventually burn and melt.

Care should be taken so that the flame does not come in direct contact with any of the ware; and the flame should be deflected by bricks, muffles, or clay saggers. If it is more convenient, the flame can be directed beneath a kiln shelf.

When designing or building a gas fired raku kiln, the size and location of the flue must be given careful consideration. Although this important aspect of the design is overlooked by many raku potters, it is a critical, if not the determining factor to successful glaze reduction. A flue opening is too large, for example, if the copper bearing glazes continually come out an oxidized green instead of a sumptuous copper looking metallic luster and remain so even after the post-firing reduction. On the other hand, a flue opening is too small if the kiln takes an unusually long time to fire to maturity and/or the pottery is covered with a dark carbon soot which can, incidentally, be burned off in three or four minutes by simply moving the kiln door or lid slightly to create a secondary flue opening. If a fixed flue size is too large and does not give good results with a particular kiln design some creative activity and experimentation may have to be done with a damper. The damper need not be anything more than a hard brick or a piece of broken kiln shelf used to cover or restrict the flue opening as needed. The damper might be used much in the same way it is used with gas fired stoneware kilns: the flue may be left uncovered during the early stages of the firing cycle to maintain an oxidizing atmosphere and rapid rise in temperature and partially or entirely covered during the final stages of the firing to obtain a reducing atmosphere within the kiln. A reducing atmosphere exists within the kiln when the flue opening is covered enough to restrict the draft or draw off oxygen at the burner port. Proper flue restriction during reduction should force a small but visible flame to

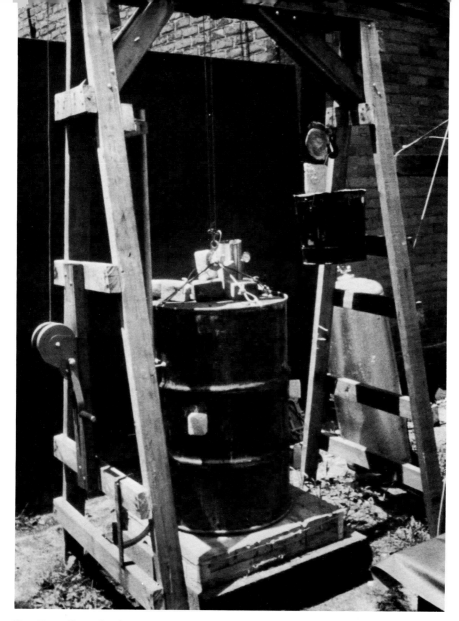

Jim Powell's raku barrel kiln suspended from a wooden frame by means of a wire cable and pulley system. The top was cast with the barrel upside down. When dry, a fiber drum, seven inches smaller in diameter, was centered in the barrel resting on the cast top and the wall insulation poured. Cardboard cylinders were positioned before casting to provide the flue, burner port, and peephole openings.

Looking into a top-loading kiln. Note the location of the burner port and the clearance between the shelf and walls.

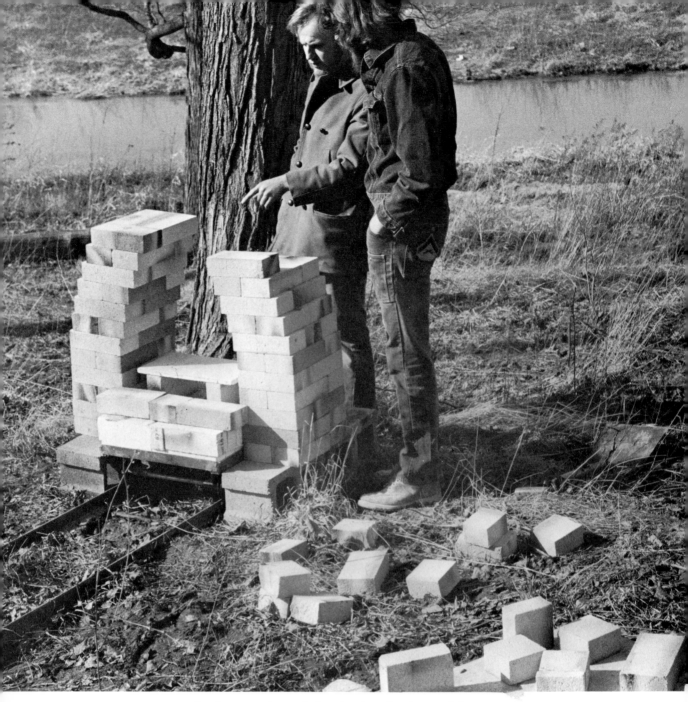

Bricking-up the corbel arch of a raku drawer kiln.

Disposable kiln shelf covers cut to size with a saber saw. Most types of asbestos boards will suffice.

2″ Dia. Flue Hole (2)

½″ x 24″ Thd. Rod (2)

5/16″ x 24″ Thd. Rod (3)

36″ Angle Iron (2)

Burner Port

G-23 Insulating Brick
(2½″ x 4½″ x 9″)

13½″

18″

2½″ High—First Tier

Wall: 9 Tiers Tall

2″ Dia. Peep Holes

(Front & Side)

Kiln Shelf
9″ x 16″

27″

22″

Note:
Two high temperature
hard bricks may be
substituted for
the kiln shelf.

6 Blk.
Foundation

Top Loading Raku Kiln

Hard Brick Shelf
and Shelf Support

Two 9″ x 18″ Hinged Doors
in Welded Angle-
Channel Iron Frame

1½″ I.D. x 7″ Pipe Hinge (2)

1¼″ O.D. x 48″ Pipe Frame

Handle

Ground Level

Exhaust

15″ D.

2″-3″ x 4½″ x 9″
Hard Brick
No. 3 Arch

Burner

4½″ Sq.

Kulasiewicz's Ground Level Raku Kiln

31½" 22½"

2½" Dia.
Flue Hole

Top:
Cast Kiln Cement-

Heavily Reinforced

3"

22½" 18"

8
7
6
5
4
3
2
1

½" x 36" Thd. Rod

8 Blk. Foundation

Side Loading Raku Kiln

Applying a protective coating of kiln shelf wash with a wide brush.

Building the top-loading kiln's removable cover. The light-weight bricks are held in place by compressions. Threaded steel rods have been placed through a hole drilled in the center of each brick and bolted to an angle iron frame.

shoot out any remaining flue opening and the burner port. Often, all that is needed for a reduction firing in a raku kiln is thirty to sixty seconds of reduction (brick over the flue) followed by thirty to sixty seconds of oxidation (flue uncovered) at the end of the firing just before the kiln is opened and the ware removed.

Reduction is not difficult to achieve in a well made fuel burning kiln. It is simply a matter of starving the kiln of oxygen. Raku kilns that are poorly made, with large openings at the joints, cannot be sufficiently reduced in that they are literally one big flue. There can be no substitute for the beautiful reduction effects that can be had in a tightly made kiln. The erratic richness and unique brilliance of the reduced glaze produces much of the most satisfying and valued raku pottery. The reduction results are most dramatic among the highly leaded or feldspathic glaze bases containing metallic colorants and, although the results can never be completely controlled, that is how it is and that in part gives each piece we make its unique presence and incarnation.

Raku car kiln making use of Frank Colson's cast catenary shell. Fiberfrax boards are used for the floor and a piece of Fiberfrax block is the flue cover. The inside of the kiln is coated with Fiberfrax cement, as are the brick joints in the movable door. A sand-cement mixture protects the outside of the shell from the elements.

6
Firing: Metamorphosis

The glaze firing is the most exciting and dramatic phase of the whole raku experience. An understanding of the fire's powers of transformation coupled with a feeling for it and its capacities is needed if one is going to realize the full potentialities of raku pottery. The raku glaze firing holds a special place of honor in the potter's craft in that it allows potters to live with and experience every transforming phase. Potters can peer into the kiln's interior and in less than an hour observe the formation of the glaze; first as it begins to sinter in the early stages of melting, then as it goes through the bubbling stage, and finally when it reaches the molten liquid state, i.e. when bubbles disappear and fusion is complete. As knowledge is gained through experience, the kiln watcher is able to make small adjustments on his ware during the firing. He might observe an unexpected bare spot on the rim and by opening the door or lid be able to drop some powdered lead or borax on it with a long handled metal dipper, or he might suddenly decide to add a powdered metallic oxide to one area for

Rita Yokoi, hanging raku planter, 15" x 7½". Fired in an electric kiln and reduced in sawdust.

Raku bottle being lifted out of the top-loading kiln by its neck. Note the broken asbestos shelf cover that is due for replacement.

additional color. Such judgments result from insights into the actions of fire and can have a direct influence on the success of a piece. Once again the opportunity of expressing ourselves creatively, even as we work with the firing, speaks of the potency of raku and its ability to reflect the wholeness of a person as he is able to express himself in all the phases of the creation of raku.

Everything—the digging of the clay; the preparation of the clay; the forming of the piece; the building of the kiln; and the firing of the bisque, is a prelude to the drama of the glaze firing. The anticipation is present in every phase of raku pottery making. When the clay body is composed, the fact that the ware will have to undergo drastic changes—going from a cold environment into a hot one, and then immediately back to a cold one—without breaking, is a consideration in the mixture of the clay body itself.

The clay body and the bisquing temperature of raku ware is determined by the final firing; if the bisque temperature is too high, the ware will lose its porosity and may break in the glaze kiln.

The shapes of the pots are created and designed for the firing. The pots must be made in shapes and sizes that will allow them to be easily placed in the kiln and removed from the kiln with tongs.

Reduction after the glaze firing is a recent American contribution to the raku process. Traditionally, the Japanese raku ware was either air-cooled or water-cooled after it was taken from the glaze kiln. This cooling process did little to alter the color of the bisque clay, and contributed little to the richness of the glaze. Most contemporary American potters either partially or fully reduce their pieces when they are removed from

Mary Town, a good example of the character and freshness in a hand-built form. The 8" high vessel was completely buried in sawdust during a ten minute post firing reduction.

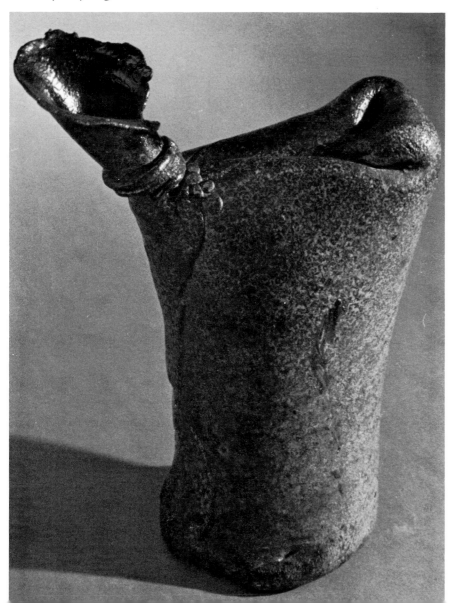

the kiln by placing them in an oxygen-free atmosphere while they are kiln-hot. The resulting reduction effects are magnificent—the clay body may turn to a smoky gray or jet black and the glazes might turn to metallic or iridescent lusters, depending on the metallic oxides or chemicals that are used.

In theory, reduction after firing is not very different from reduction during firing, as is often done with high fire fuel—burning stoneware kilns. When oxygen is in short supply, carbon and carbon monoxide are liberated during combustion and they chemically take oxygen from any other available source—such as the clay and the glaze materials. These materials are "reduced" when they are deprived of oxygen and the reduction affects their color. Reduction, as associated with raku is usually a post firing treatment and is done at low temperatures allowing for a wide range of glaze colors that are not possible at high firing stoneware temperatures. The time involved is also very short so that the results are only on the surface in contrast to the penetrating effects in the reduction of stoneware.

I've tried reducing raku ware in the kiln during the glaze firing by inserting moth balls through the peep holes and by blocking off the secondary air supply at the burner port and plugging up the primary air supply on the burner with clay. In both cases there were billows of black smoke, but only slightly noticeable reduction effects could be seen on the pieces. A partial reduction atmosphere can best be had inside the kiln by controlling the size of the flue opening during the firing.

For post firing glaze reduction to be effective the glaze must undergo some reduction during the firing. This is best achieved in a tightly bricked kiln with a relatively small flue opening. If glaze reduction is not being achieved during the firing of an existing kiln chances are the flue opening is too large, in which case a brick may be used to restrict it slightly. Although a small flue will lengthen the firing time it is nevertheless a helpful solution to the problem of glaze reduction.

Robert Piepenburg, globular raku jar, 10" high. The alternating variations in the glaze color are primarily the result of a reduction atmosphere in the kiln during the firing.

Robert Piepenburg, hanging raku form, 10" x 20". The steel stampings, which were embedded in the wet clay, do not melt at the low glazing temperatures of raku.

Robert Piepenburg, slab built raku and mirror wall form, 3" x 25". The mirror serves to expose the other side of the slabs and add visual depth.

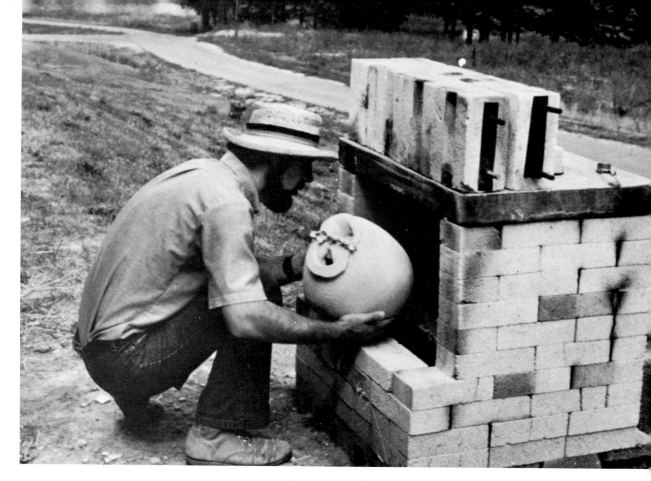

Loading a cold kiln.

Loading the Kiln

The glaze firing can be a success only if the glaze melts and covers properly. The way the glaze is applied is determined by the firing. If a large section of the body is left unglazed, the reduced clay should turn black complimenting the surrounding glazed areas.

Glaze dampness causes more breakage during the firing than does any other single factor. Air bubbles in the clay and excessive thickness of the clay walls are often cited as factors in breakage, but to my knowledge they seldom, if ever, cause pieces to explode in the raku kiln. Poor construction and an overfired bisque also account for some breakage. The best way to keep pots from blowing up during the glaze firing is to make sure that they are absolutely dry before they are placed in the glaze kiln. The vehicle for glaze is water, and it must evaporate completely before the firing. Usually, the glaze must be applied at least a day before the firing of the kiln. If a piece were glazed just before it was placed in the

Whipping powdered tea and hot water in a raku bowl.

kiln, it would almost certainly be damp, and would probably explode during the firing.

Some potters put their newly glazed ware into an electric bisque kiln leaving the lid open and the electric switches turned to low for about an hour before placing them into a hot raku kiln. Other potters pre-heat their glazed pots for several hours by placing them on top of a kiln that is being fired. Other potters include them in the first firing of a cold kiln, bringing the temperature up slowly. These methods are not completely

Placing ware into a top loading kiln. Tongs designed by author for tumescent ware.

Lighting the burner.

satisfactory and I suggest you simply allow the glaze to dry overnight, or even longer if the weather is rainy or humid. After the glaze is dry, it certainly won't hurt to place the ware on the top of the hot or firing kiln for pre-heating as the pieces await firing. Pre-heating is not really necessary, but if no ware-board, or shelf for glaze ware storage, is available it is safer to store the ware on the top of a kiln than leave the glazed ware on the ground where it might pick up moisture, or be stepped on.

If by chance, a piece should explode and you hear it, open the kiln immediately and remove all the fragments. If other pots are being fired, the debris might fall and fuse to them, ruining everything in the kiln.

Pieces that are large, awkward to handle, fragile, or made from a stoneware body should be included in a first firing of a cold kiln. With bare hands, the pieces can be easily placed in the best position, thereby decreasing the chances for breakage by the tongs. Careful positioning of a piece also decreases the chances for breakage when the piece is removed with the tongs. A slow, gradual rise in temperature is also easier on most ware, particularly large pieces that have been constructed of many slabs that have been joined into one large piece.

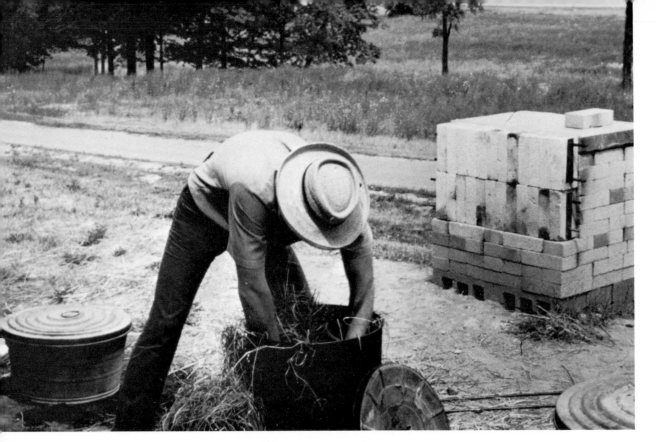

Filling reduction container with hay.

In loading the kiln you may find some pieces that have to be propped up with a brick, or leaned against the kiln wall. If a piece touches another pot, no great harm will result because the glaze will be fluid when the pots are taken from the kiln and the pieces will separate easily.

Platters, tiles, and flat pieces are best fired standing on edge and leaning against the inside wall of the kiln. They take up less room and are easily removed from this position. However, unusual glaze patterns might result from a running glaze, and you should be prepared for them. It is also much safer to fire large flat forms on end or propped up against a wall rather than resting flat on a shelf—particularly in a hot kiln. Kilns that have been firing for several hours, or whose lower shelves are near a combustion chamber become very hot and can cause cracking in and near the bottoms of the ware. Placing glazed pieces on a glowing hot shelf is too much of a heat shock for the new, cold ware. A solution for this problem is to pre-heat the ware or change the shelves, replace the glowing hot ones with preheated shelves that are slightly cooler. You couldn't use cold shelves because they would crack or blow up since they, too, would suffer from the thermal shock. The best solution is to shut the kiln down and allow it to cool for an hour or so.

Different glazes will melt at different temperatures and you must make sure that all of the bubbles have disappeared before it is removed from the kiln. In most cases the bubbles will remain when the piece is cooled. At times it is wise to let a piece at the fluid-glaze stage remain in the kiln an extra minute or two at a constant temperature before removing it; this will assure uniform maturity. Depending upon the circumstances, glaze will usually melt on the inside bottom of the piece first and on the upper rim last. If the glaze is applied too thickly to a bowl form, it will puddle inside on the bottom; when that happens place the hot bowl on a level surface so that the glaze puddle will not cool and harden at an angle.

In firing a number of pieces, the kiln should be unloaded and reloaded again as quickly as possible. Working quickly saves fuel and time, and keeps the kiln at an even heat. Each succeeding load will require less time and less fuel. When the kiln is very hot a firing cycle may take as little as ten or fifteen minutes.

Securing the kiln.

Removing a two-piece door.

Removing pot from a hot kiln.

The Firing Cycle

The time required for the initial firing of a cold kiln depends on the size or type of kiln to be used. In most cases it should take less than an hour. If a piece is unusually large or complicated it might be placed in a cold kiln and fired slowly up to temperature over a period of two or three hours before being removed or reduced in place. Porcelain can even be fired successfully in this manner. The real thermo-shock to raku ware comes when a relatively cold piece is loaded into a hot kiln and not, as many believe, when the piece is brought from the kiln into a cold atmosphere.

In using vaporized propane for fuel I start firing with a pressure of ten pounds and after several firings, when the bricks have heated I usually lower the pressure to anywhere from four to six pounds. When loading or unloading, the pressure is turned down even further, either at the regulator on the tank, or better still, at the needle valve on the burner, allowing just enough pressure to keep the flame from going out. This not only saves fuel that might otherwise be wasted in an open kiln, but it is safer, and much pleasanter than working near a continuously blasting wave of invisible heat.

Kiln shelves need to be removed and cleaned frequently, especially if you want a clean, well-reduced foot area on your pots instead of a foot that is caked with several different glazes and in need of grinding. If glaze does puddle on the kiln shelf, sand or grog can be sprinkled over the patch of glaze before the kiln is loaded. If hard bricks are used for a shelf, and become covered with glaze, they may be easily discarded and inexpensively replaced with clean new ones.

Using Tongs

Long handled tongs are generally used for removing the red hot glazed ware and for the placement of unfired glaze ware into the hot kiln. The tongs can be made from metal tubing, flat iron, iron rod, pipe, or any material that is handy or usable. The tongs that I use are fabricated from

Hand-forged raku tongs with thirty-six inch handles. The tongs with the three inch round jaws are designed and sold by Robert Piepenburg, Ann Arbor, Michigan.

hand-forged iron rod three-eighths of an inch thick. They have round jaws that are three inches in diameter and handles that are three feet long. I designed these tongs to be light and easy to work with, and I'm particularly proud that they are made by one of the last real blacksmiths in the Detroit area.

Tongs are simple to fashion and you can probably make your own. In fact, it may become necessary at times to design and make a unique device for removing unusual forms from a kiln. They can be made to work like scissors if you attach two pieces of metal with a bolt and nut at some common point. The prongs or jaw ends should touch when closed and be fashioned to easily hold a three- to six-inch diameter cylinder when opened. Even fireplace tongs would be suitable, if one can find a way of extending their handles.

Asbestos gloves can be used to hold the tongs, especially if you use a top loading kiln. Heat rises; when a top loading kiln is opened, you can easily burn your hands even when the very long-handled tongs are used. Asbestos gloves are also useful for picking up and moving still warm ware at the kiln's site, for lifting hot bucket lids, for adding a tier of bricks to raise the wall of a hot kiln, or to simply prevent burnt fingers.

The Reduction

The special aura that permeates the raku experience centers about the firing and yields itself to us at that moment when we reach into the open kiln with our tongs. That moment, more than any of the other growth stages of the raku pot, has the potential of revealing and truthfully illuminating our inner selves. In the few seconds that it takes to pick up the pot with tongs and remove the pot from the kiln, all the potter's experiences are directed at the ware and all are summoned into consciousness. All the preparation and previous activity are evaluated in terms of what is done in the next few moments. The personal commitment of the potter to his work and to himself is reflected in the way the potter handles each piece of raku while it is glowing in the jaws of the tongs.

Pieces that are going to be heavily reduced must be immediately taken from the hot kiln and quickly placed into an air-tight enclosure containing some dry combustibles. Sawdust, excelsior, shredded paper, leaves, and straw might be used as combustibles, and only a few handfuls of one of these materials is needed. The most effective air-tight enclosure is a hole dug in the ground and covered with an inverted metal trash can, or just the lid of the trash can, depending on the size of the piece to be reduced.

If a reduction container is not completely air tight or a great deal larger than the ware, a large quantity of one of the dry combustibles is needed. The combustible material is placed at the bottom of the hole and the just-from-the-kiln piece is put in the hole on top of the sawdust, leaves, etc. The cover of the can is quickly placed over the top of the can or hole, making an air-tight enclosure and sealing the piece within. Additional combustibles such as straw or hay may be thrown on top of the ware, especially if there are large unglazed areas, and allowed to ignite before

the cover is added. The results of the reduction depend greatly on the condition of the combustible material that is used; if the material is damp, coarse, or used, it will not burn well, nor provide much free carbon. However, the results of reduction done in a covered pit are usually strong and excellent because an almost completely air-tight seal is formed by the cover of the can and the ground, and any oxygen is prevented from entering the hole and weakening the reduction.

Clay bodies turn a rich black and glazes with colorants turn to dark lusters in the smoky atmosphere. Some glazes become too dark and lustery in the pit and are better looking if they are held in the air for a few moments and allowed to oxidize and cool slightly before being reduced. Other glazes look best when not reduced at all and are left to oxidize on an open pile of sawdust so that just the exposed clay at the bottom of the piece gets a partial reduction.

It is sometimes wise to leave ware enclosed in the reducing atmosphere for about five to ten minutes while the ware cools. The glaze reduction will take place immediately, but the piece might re-oxidize and the reduction effects partially lost if the piece were allowed to cool in the open air after being reduced for only a short period of time. To avoid re-oxidation many potters quench their ware with water immediately after removing it from the reducing atmosphere. It is a technique I seldom use because of the large amount of breakage caused by the additional shock of the dunking in cold water. For good and lasting glaze reductions raku pottery must be allowed to cool in the reduction atmosphere.

Interesting reduction effects can be achieved by burying a piece of ware either partially or entirely under a combustible fuel such as sawdust. If you use this technique it is usually a good idea to have the reduction fuel, especially sawdust, slightly damp, or combine with sawdust that has been reclaimed from another glaze firing session. This will not only prevent the entire container of sawdust from flaming up, but it will also prevent an over-reduced glaze from becoming charred and blackened. The dark pocky roughness of sawdust impressions can be unpleasant, although the impressions of the patterns made by burned-out grass or leaves might be very attractive and desirable. A note of caution: liquid molten glaze that is buried with or comes into contact with the reducing material will develop charred textures that can be rough and unattractive.

Sometimes I lightly mix a thin motor oil with the sawdust to wet it down, and to bring out special lusters in the glaze. This works well with many glazes, especially those containing copper oxide. The one big disadvantage of using an oil treated combustible, other than that it is danger-

udent taking a pot from the kiln to a reduction barrel. Note the whiteness
the clay on the bottom of the pot. If the pot were to be quenched in
ter before being reduced in a closed container it would remain white and
t turn the smoky black color that is characteristic of contemporary raku.

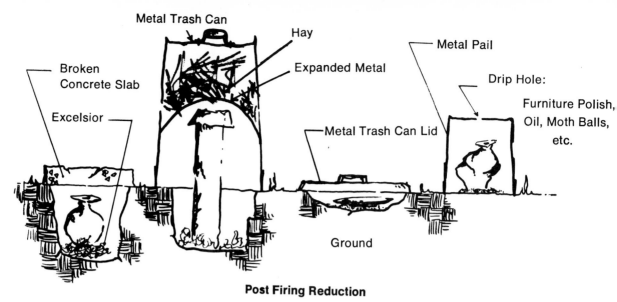

Broken Concrete Slab

Excelsior

Metal Trash Can

Hay

Expanded Metal

Metal Trash Can Lid

Metal Pail

Drip Hole:

Furniture Polish, Oil, Moth Balls, etc.

Ground

Post Firing Reduction

Water

Open Sawdust Pile

Oil Soaked Sawdust

Oil Soaked Burlap

Ground

Filling reduction containers with sawdust.

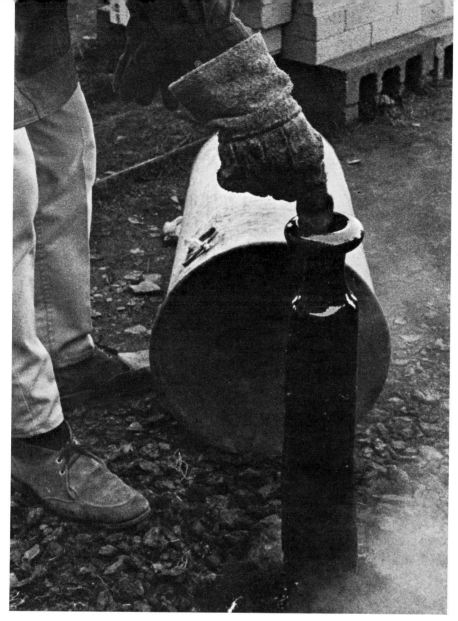

An extra tall container was used in the post firing reduction of this form by the author.

Combustibles: shredded paper, excelsior, and fine sawdust (in the plastic bag).

Filling reduction containers with grass clippings and sawdust.

Heavy smoked reductions are best obtained in pits of dry sawdust covered with air tight lids.

Reducing the bottom portion of form in an open pile of sawdust.

Reducing forms in an open pile of leaves.

Reducing in hay.

Unloading a kiln containing a small bowl, a large cylindrical form, and a platter fired on edge. In up-draft kilns the bottoms of the forms get more heat than the rims.

Removing the cooled pot from reduction container.

Examining reduction effects.

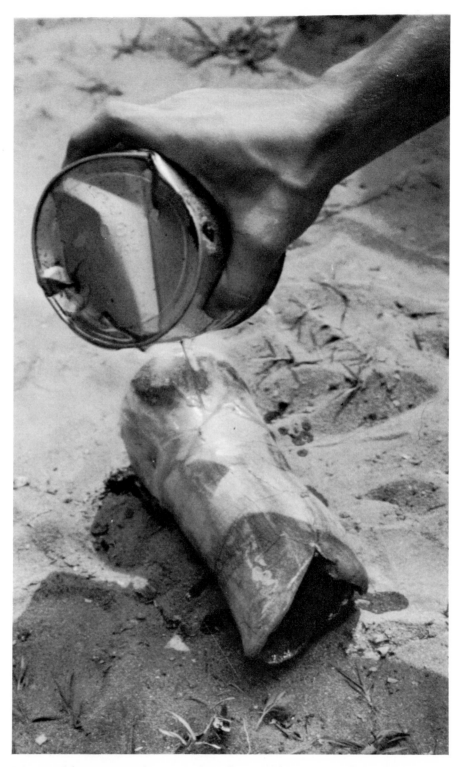

Motor oil being poured on a cooling, but still hot, form. This enhances and deepens the crackles in the glaze. Liquid furniture polish will sometimes work better than oil.

ously flammable, is it is difficult to clean up the ware after it has cooled. The slippery, oily coating on the glazed surface should be removed and if a steel wool soap pad is used one has to be careful so as not to scour away any patina-luster-like areas of glaze.

When glaze has matured and the ware is ready to be taken from the kiln you must make the decisions that will ultimately affect the final appearance of the form. Needless to say, no one else should ever fire your work. Not only would it oppose the spirit of raku, but it would deny the final moments of intimacy between the pot and the potter that culminate the creative experience.

The possibilities for raku pottery effects are many and new approaches will always develop as pot and potter grow and change through the experience of the fire. The uncertainties are many and fire can symbolize the warmth of love, or the wrath of an inferno. We, as potters, often stand humble before the power of the fire with all of our hopes both melting away and burning with anticipation, as they lie flickering in the flames of suspense. And, best of all, if the results are disappointing or unsatisfactory, the piece may be reglazed while it is still hot, and with crossed fingers, and high hopes, we can surrender it once again to the flames.

Bud McKee having a solution of iron chloride, alcohol, and water sprayed on his non-copper glaze. This is done before undergoing the post-firing reduction for an iron luster. This photo was taken on the beach at Pescadero, California, where rakuists have been coming together for over ten years to share the beach environment and ideas/feelings about raku. The three-day event is sponsored by the San Francisco State University Art Department Ceramics Area.

Epilogue

I hope this book will not only serve further the needs of those who make raku pottery but will also bring information and awareness to those who have not yet attempted the technique.

There is much for the individual to experience and ponder on in raku. The experiences are as much internal as they are external. The interrelatedness of man, material, and process may on occasion give birth to a uniquely beautiful pot and this is good. But that which binds the potter to raku is not a finished pot, anymore than a child is the only thing that binds a man and a woman. It is the accompanying experiences and transformations that serve as a continuous and binding force. A force that is unsummoned. A force that can lead to new acts of artistic expression and ways of living.

It is this formative force that, to me, is characteristic of the raku experience; the resultant pottery is of secondary importance. It is not, therefore, coincidental or ironical to find much of raku pottery infused with an invisible, loving, sensitive, and often imaginative spirit. Awareness is inherent to the realm of raku. If we are aware of the moment, aware of ourselves, we, as well as our pots, will have content.

To be aware and to live with a traveling mind is to bring one's uniqueness to fruition. The artist today is becoming one of America's modern heroes. In our contemporary heterogenous society where there are fewer and fewer socially maintained group rites and values he becomes the new spiritual guide. When individual self-expression is a culturally accepted undertaking, the artist, by communicating his own experiences and inner quests, becomes the new hero. His Odyssey, like the adventures of heroes in mythology, aids modern man in his search for meaning. There are times when we feel despair rather than fulfillment in our work; this is often due to a lack of kinship between material, form, and expression. When this happens, pots become just words and not poems. Delight and comfort is taken with "traditional" forms with no search made for poetic ones. Why do we neglect our passion? Why not sponsor our personal feeling, our experience, our birth cry?

Clay was freight.
Miracle was the fertilization of dead matter.
Reflection was a provoker.
Vision was a consequence.
Struggle was nourishment.
Invention was fiction.
Independence was ironical.
Eden was technique.
Failure was conceitment.
The SOUL was the hero.
Theme was image.
Craft was breeze.
Tradition a lie.
Respectful attention notwithstanding.
Dialogue with the self, with the clay he made a pot.

Safety
Precautions

Pottery is not a dangerous activity, but as with anything else, accidents can happen if you are not alert to possible hazards, and if you do not employ safety precautions at all times. Accidents can be caused by the nature and condition of the equipment and facilities, or by personal practices, or by both. As a teacher I have always tried to recognize hazards for the purpose of eliminating or minimizing them, and of mollifying their effects. But more importantly, I have come to realize the importance of having a positive attitude toward being safe. If the desire to be safe exists at all times—even during those moments of eagerness inherent to raku pottery—injury can be prevented. Safety, like making good pottery, requires awareness. Many hazards, nevertheless, exist and are included here so that you may be aware of them, and take the necessary preventative precautions. Forewarned is forearmed.

Lead Glazes

The lead base glazes used by many raku potters present a hazard with respect to personal health and safety. If the lead base glazes are frequently used, they should be handled with extreme caution and care should be taken so that the lead, or the lead glaze is not placed on surfaces which might be used, at any time or in any way, for food or drink.

The glaze should not come into contact with your skin and the dust vapors should not be inhaled. This includes the possible inhaling of lead particles that might be circulating in the air from the use of a spray gun, or the particles that might be inhaled while in the vicinity of the kiln flue opening (lead fumes are expelled by lead glazes during the firing).

To avoid undesirable vapors, gases, and smoke, lead glaze firings should be done outdoors. The kiln should be located where there is a good supply of fresh circulating air. A small outdoor patio, enclosed on all sides, but with no roof, is inadequate and incapable of quickly dispersing heavy reduction smoke.

Propane Gas

Burners should be lit the instant the gas is turned on. When lighting the burner, hold it in your hand, and away from the burner port. Should the wind, or some other chance happening cause the burner to go out, the kiln should be purged of any gas before relighting. Remember, propane gas, unlike natural gas, is heavier than air and will cling to the kiln floor and not dissipate immediately by going out of an upper flue.

Exploding Ware Inside the Kiln

If, during the firing, a damp pot should begin to explode, the kiln should be opened and the broken fragments removed before they fuse to other pots. However, do this with extreme caution: sometimes pieces will suddenly come shooting out of the open kiln at a great velocity. Above all, do not look into the peep hole to see what has happened. Peep holes, like flue openings, are dangerous because they emit strong but invisible heat waves that are capable of injuring the eye or singeing the eyebrows or hair of an eager but incautious potter.

Post Firing Reduction

When placing ware in containers for post firing reduction, be on the lookout for possible flame-ups. Combustibles, particularly dry or oil treated sawdust, will ignite instantly on contact with the glowing ware. These combustibles can send up dangerous flames as well as billows of blinding smoke.

Care should be taken when opening an air-tight reduction container. The inrush of air will, in some cases, re-ignite the combustible material in the bottom of the hole or can, and flames will shoot out.

Kiln Site

Fires also can flare up at the kiln site. They usually come from careless handling of hot fired ware, especially if the kiln is located in a field of dry grass and not in a sandy area. Clear the dry brush and grass from the kiln area before building and firing the kiln.

Hair

Long hair is best tied back or tucked under your collar or other clothing at the back of your neck.

Clothing

Loose clothing anywhere can be a problem; I have seen baggy sweater sleeves and baggy pants cuffs catch fire. It is a good idea to have a heavy wool or asbestos fire-blanket nearby and handy whenever you are firing your kiln.

Bare Feet

Bare feet, like exposed legs or arms, present additional risks for the potter. Shoes and jeans protect the potter from painful and harmful burns.

Sandals should not be worn around the kiln or reduction area. Hot and burning sparks, cinders, or ashes may get caught and trapped between the toes or between the sandals and the feet.

Hands

To protect the fingers and hands from burns which frequently come from the irresistible impulse to touch the still-hot pots or kilns, asbestos gloves or mittens are a necessity. When holes burn through the gloves or the gloves wear out, they should be replaced immediately.

For those who are alert, hazards can be seen and overcome. Like life, there is no blueprint to safety—one must simply do the best he can, not only for himself but for everyone.

Related Bibliography

Berensohn, Paulus. *Finding One's Way with Clay*. New York: Simon and Schuster, 1972.

Dickerson, John. *Raku Handbook*. New York: Van Nostrand Reinhold Co., 1972.

Leach, Bernard H. *A Potter's Book*. Levittown, N.Y.: Transatlantic Arts, Inc., 1965.

Lee, Sherman E. *Tea Taste In Japanese Art*. Greenwich, Conn.: Asia House Gallery, 1963.

Nagumo, Ryu. *Japanese Pottery As a Hobby*. San Francisco: Japan Publications Trading Center, 1963.

Nakamura, Julia V. *The Japanese Tea Ceremony*. Mount Vernon, N.Y.: The Peter Pauper Press, 1965.

Okakura, Kakuzo. *The Book of Tea*. New York: Dover Publications, Inc., 1964.

Rhodes, Daniel. *Clay and Glazes for the Potter*. Philadelphia: Chilton, 1973.

———. *Kilns: Design, Construction, and Operation*. Philadelphia: Chilton, 1958.

———. *Tamba Pottery: The Timeless Art of a Japanese Village*. Palo Alto, Calif.: Kodansha International/USA, Ltd., 1970.

Richards, Mary C. *Centering In Pottery, Poetry, and the Person*. Middletown, Conn.: Wesleyan University Press, 1964.

Riegger, Hal. *Raku, Art and Technique*. New York: Van Nostrand Reinhold Co., 1970.

Sadler, A. L. *Cha-No-Yu, The Japanese Tea Ceremony*. Rutland, Vermont: Charles E. Tuttle Co., 1970.

Sanders, Herbert H. *The World of Japanese Ceramics*. Palo Alto, Calif.: Kodansha International/USA, Ltd., 1967.

Tyler, Christopher, and Richard Hirsch. *Raku*. New York: Watson-Guptill Publications, 1975.

Photo Credits

All photographs and illustrations by Robert Piepenburg except:

Neil Atkins: 62, 63, 64, 70, 76, 109 (bottom), 117 (bottom), 126, 140, 141 (top)
Harley Foxworthy: 25, 51, 55 (left), 68, 78, 127
Richard Wood: 38
David Keyes: 41
Ko-on: 43, 44
Morse Collection, Museum of Fine Arts, Boston: 37, 45
Sandor B. Brent: 46
Sister Celeste Mary Bourke: 48
Loren Bivens: 71
Paul Soldner: 29, 31, 103
David Middlebrook: 54, 56 (left), 104
Frank Colson: 105 (top left), 123
Hank Murrow: 113
Hal Riegger: 108 (top)
Frank Kulasiewicz: 108 (bottom)
Rita Yokoi: 125
Kathie Hund: ii (first color insert)
Wayne Higby: 57, 58 (top)
Ruth Ellen Hollingsworth: 58 (bottom), 96 (bottom)
Steven Kemenyffy: 97
Jim Powell: 74
Seattle Art Museum: 18 (bottom)
Oakland Community College, Orchid Ridge Campus: 72, 102 (top), 105 (bottom
   left), 112, 142 (top), 146
Ray Kahmeyer: 16
Ken Hendry: 17
Nancy Jurs: 18 (top)
Bill Stewart: 23
Angelo C. Garzio: 26
Daniel Rhodes: 40
George Timock: 47
Anne Kingsbury: 79
Marie Carter: 102 (bottom)
Kurt Weiser: 105 (right)

Index